LOVE LETTERS

Tips to Make Your Marriage Better from A-Z

By: Reginald & Kelley Steele

STEELE STRONG PUBLISHING

Arizona, USA
2024

Copyright © 2024 by Reginald & Kelley Steele

All rights reserved. No part of this book may be reproduced in any form on by any electronic or mechanical means, including information storage and retrieval systems, without permission in writing from the publisher, except by a reviewer who may quote brief passages in a review.

Book Cover by DG Premier Design Studio
Illustrations by DG Premier Design Studio
First printing edition 2024

ISBN: 979-8-9915176-2-1

www.kelleysteele.com

Pastors Reginald & Kelley Steele

Married for 30 Years and counting......

Dedication

This book is dedicated to husbands and wives who are committed to their relationship. We want to encourage you to grow in your marriage by providing simple tips that are retainable and applicable. These are not just words, they are things we've learned and applied throughout our relationship.

Providing three words for each letter of the alphabet is our way of simplifying marital guidance that couples can adhere to. It is our prayer for you that this book becomes a regular tool that you turn to. We have also provided activities that will teach you to live out each definition.

This book is our way for you and the one you love to last from A - Z.

A

AFFIRM

Expressing your belief in his role as a husband is a powerful way to affirm your dedication to him. Speaking positively about him to others is another way to declare his valued place in your life.

While he may not ask for it, he often needs emotional support, especially when facing challenging circumstances. Being the positive voice in his life reassures him that you are in his corner.

Even the strongest man needs to hear he is strong—from the woman he loves. 1 Thessalonians 5:11 says to encourage one another and build each other up. Affirming your husband allows you to do both!

APPRECIATE

Appreciate your wife and recognize the immense value she brings into your life. When you fully recognize her worth, you'll understand her significance in your journey together.

She is there to fill a void, to complete the missing piece that brings you a sense of wholeness. Make her feel seen by acknowledging her contributions and efforts.

This will boost her morale, motivate her to keep going, and strengthen her resilience, reducing stress with the simple words, "I appreciate you." Psalm 118:24 encourages us to do good for one another.
How much more so for a husband and wife?

ATTENTION

Attending to your wife means to be willing to deal with her, especially her emotions. Emotional attendance consists of being present and in the moment. An understanding ear and a warm embrace can go a long way for a wife who is feeling overwhelmed.

As a husband, being attentive means you are watchful and perceptive. It means that you are alert and ready to respond to a possible threat or harm toward the one you love. She will feel guarded and protected. A woman that feels safe is a secure woman.

A

Activities

APPRECIATE: "A GRATITUDE LETTER"

Activity: Dedicate an evening to writing "A Gratitude Letter" to your spouse. Highlight specific actions, qualities, or moments that have stood out recently. Share examples, such as how they supported you during a tough time or brought joy to your day. Exchange and read the letters aloud to each other.

Why It Uplifts: Gratitude fosters positivity and ensures your spouse feels valued for their contributions.

How It Reinforces Bonds: This activity strengthens trust and reminds both partners of the importance of their relationship, fostering mutual appreciation and connection.

AFFIRM: "THE PUBLIC PRAISE"

Activity: At a family or social gathering, publicly praise your spouse. Mention specific qualities or accomplishments, such as their hard work, kindness, or dedication. Ensure your compliment is heartfelt and genuine, highlighting something that truly reflects your admiration for them.

Why It Boosts Confidence: Public praise builds your spouse's self-esteem and demonstrates your respect and appreciation for their efforts.

How It Shows Pride: Sharing admiration in front of others reinforces their value in your life and deepens the sense of partnership.

ATTENTIVE: "THE LISTENING HOUR"

Activity: Create a space where your spouse feels they have your undivided attention. Spend 30 minutes in a distraction-free environment, actively listening to their thoughts, feelings, or concerns. Practice active listening by making eye contact, nodding, and summarizing their words to confirm understanding.

Why It Deepens Intimacy: Active listening fosters emotional closeness and makes your spouse feel valued and understood.

How It Prevents Misunderstandings: Being fully present minimizes miscommunication and strengthens your foundation of trust and understanding.

B

BUILD

A wife is a natural builder. She was created to strengthen her husband; to add to, not take away. Her natural instincts merge with supernatural wisdom that can establish a home and cause everything and everyone in it to prosper.

She has a way of bonding with her man that develops a long-term connection that will last from generation to generation. She is willing to construct a stable life alongside her husband. Solid is her work ethic; firm is her faith.

BELIEVE

When a husband knows his wife believes in him, he feels as if there is almost nothing he cannot accomplish. Having confidence in his ability, with or without proof, will eventually produce evidence to back her opinion. It is the certainty of his wife that pushes him to produce and stand firmly in his purpose.

When the difficult task is conquered and the victory won, he will look at his wife as the one who never wavered but always believed in him.

BEND

When a husband can bend, he is one who directs or turns his wife's outlook or expectation in a certain direction. Without manipulation, he should be able to make the hard decisions that benefit the family. This is a type of leadership that may be needed from time to time.

It is during difficult situations or challenging circumstances that he may have to convince his wife to trust his directions and agree with him, even if reluctantly. A husband and wife who can bend together will never break.

B

Activities

BUILD: "THE FOUNDATION LETTER"

Activity: Write a letter highlighting the qualities and moments that have built the strength of your relationship. Share specific examples of their love, support, or actions, and read the letters aloud together during a quiet moment.

Why It Strengthens Bonds: Reflecting on these "building blocks" reinforces trust, gratitude, and unity.

How It Encourages Connection: Acknowledging what fortifies your relationship deepens emotional closeness and partnership.

BELIEVE: "DREAM SUPPORT PLAN"

Activity: Create a "Dream Support Plan" with your spouse. Share one personal or shared goal you each want to achieve, and brainstorm ways you can actively support one another. Write down a pledge affirming your belief in their abilities and discuss how you'll encourage each other on this journey.

Why It Inspires Growth: Expressing belief in your spouse's goals boosts their confidence and affirms their dreams are valued.

How It Deepens Trust: Supporting each other's ambitions demonstrates a partnership built on mutual respect and encouragement.

BEND: "THE FLEXIBILITY CHALLENGE"

Activity: Practice a "Flexibility Challenge" by taking turns planning an activity or day your spouse enjoys, even if it's out of your comfort zone. Discuss the experience afterward, focusing on what you learned about their interests and joy.

Why It Builds Understanding: This activity encourages compromise and empathy, strengthening emotional intimacy.

How It Shows Dedication: Willingness to step out of your comfort zone for your spouse highlights your commitment to their happiness.

C

CONSISTENCY

A wife who is consistent is one who is unchanging in nature and stable in her standards. Her husband knows her behavior and can anticipate her actions, which ultimately builds confidence and connection within the relationship.

Always willing to grow—yet from a place grounded in her values—she is motivated to keep a steady rhythm in her home that's easy to follow. She keeps her word and expects the same in return. Because her husband can depend on her, she can depend on him.

Galatians 6:9 reminds us not to grow weary in doing good, for in due season we will reap if we do not give up. A wife who remains steadfast in doing good will surely reap a harvest.

CELEBRATE

When a husband is celebrated, he feels honored for his actions. No man wants more than his wife to sing his praises, especially for accomplishments. Showing admiration by doing something special, even if small, expresses acknowledgment and approval.

When a man feels admired, he can sense respect. A wife who respects her husband and celebrates him often will feel cherished and loved. Proverbs 5:18 says to rejoice with the wife of your youth. This rejoicing should be enjoyed by the couple. No one wants to celebrate anything alone, so it's best to recognize the wins of life, both big and small, together.

COMPROMISE

A wife who can compromise is a woman who is willing to settle a dispute. Meeting her husband halfway is not a posture of defeat, but one of concession. Her making the decision to agree to a happy medium instead of holding her ground can derail dissension and avoid arguments.

One of the most common compromises is agreeing to disagree. When the wife and husband understand that not seeing eye-to-eye on everything does not have to cause contention in the marriage is compromising at its' best.

C

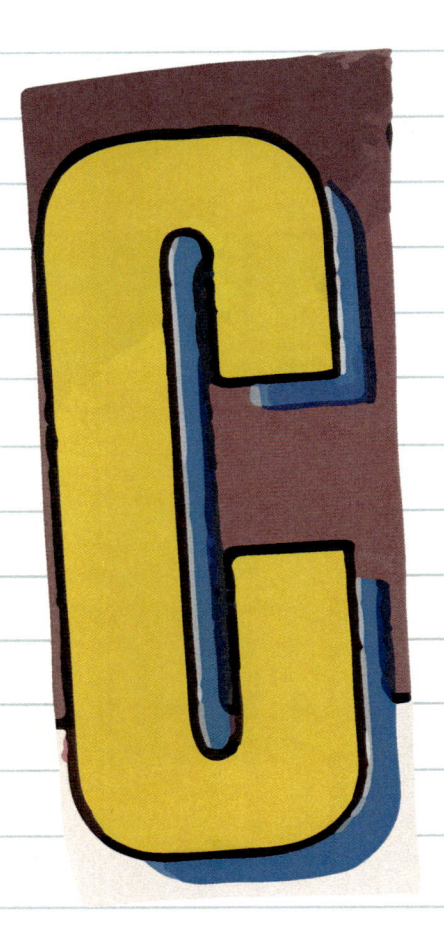

Activities

CONSISTENCY: "DAILY CONNECTION ROUTINE"

Activity: Set a "Daily Connection Routine." Agree on one consistent action each day, such as sharing a meal, saying a prayer together, or a goodnight hug. Keep this routine even during busy times.

Why It Strengthens Trust: Regular, predictable actions create stability and a dependable rhythm in your relationship.

How It Builds Partnership: Showing consistency reinforces reliability, making both spouses feel secure and valued.

CELEBRATE: "SURPRISE GRATITUDE MOMENT"

Activity: Plan a "Surprise Gratitude Moment." Write down your spouses recent accomplishments or qualities you admire. Present these in a meaningful way—through a dinner toast, a handwritten note, or a small gift.

Why It Fosters Joy: Celebrating achievements creates shared happiness and deepens emotional intimacy.

How It Encourages Positivity: Recognizing victories, big or small, fosters mutual appreciation and strengthens the bond.

COMPROMISE: "THE DECISION-SWAP DAY"

Activity: Try a "Decision-Swap Day." For a day, take turns deciding on compromises for minor choices (e.g., what to eat, activities to do). End the day reflecting on how it felt to prioritize each other's preferences.

Why It Promotes Understanding: Actively practicing give-and-take builds respect for each other's perspectives.

How It Prevents Conflict: Encouraging flexibility reduces tension and fosters teamwork in resolving differences.

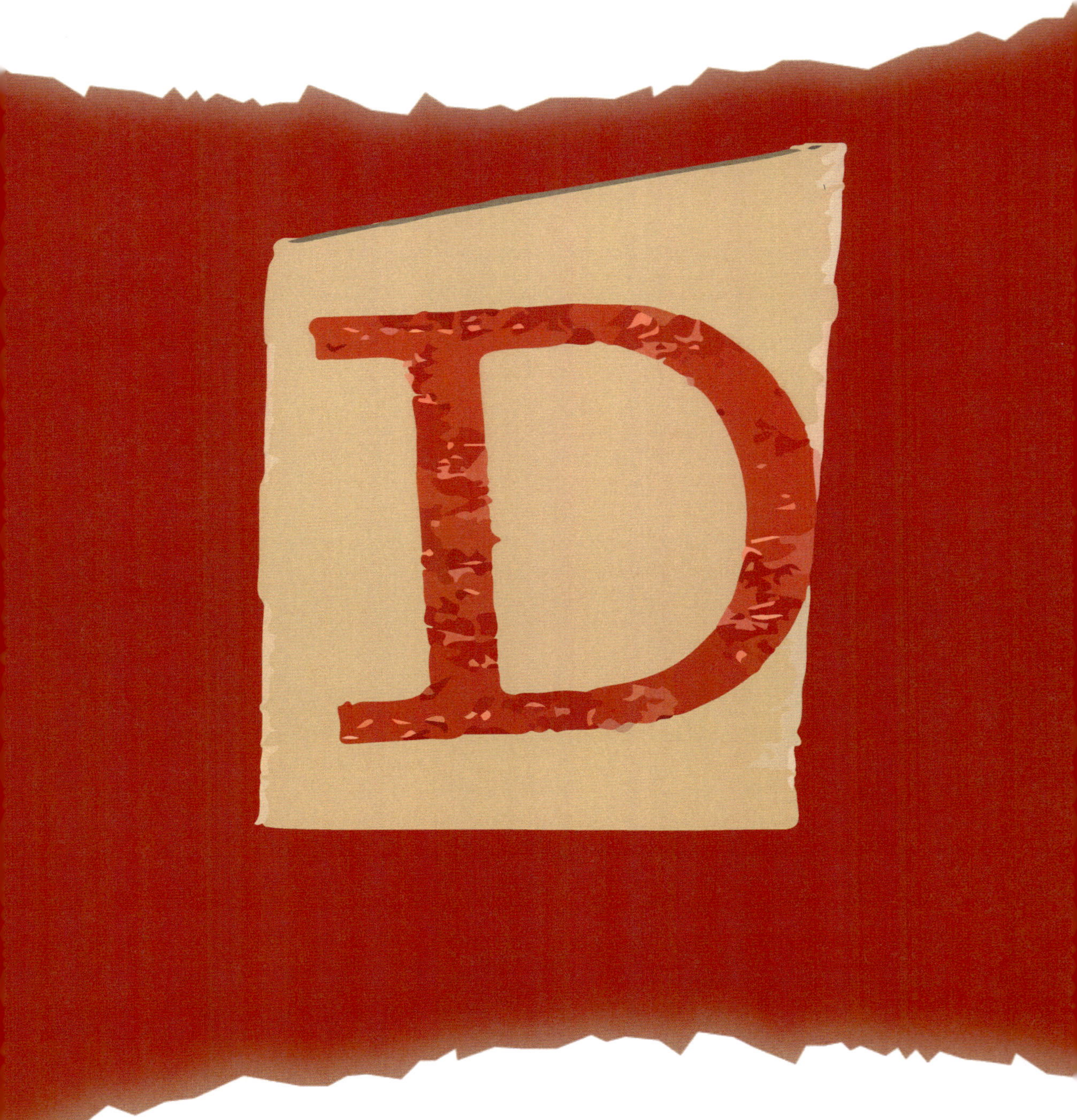
D

DEDICATION

When a husband is dedicated to his wife, he willingly gives her his time and energy because she is important to him. He carves time out of his daily schedule not out of obligation, but out of commitment. His wife knows that his allegiance is to her and their family.

She will not wonder if tough times will cause him to retreat from his responsibilities; he will not fade away when faced with difficult circumstances. A dedicated husband is willing to work through issues with his wife. His loyalty nurtures a strong, healthy relationship that can last a lifetime.

DATING

It doesn't matter if it's the wife or the husband who plans a night out—it's something that should be done often. Dating is more than just the romantic aspect of spending time together; it's an essential part of maintaining your connection as a couple. It should be a regular practice in your marriage, not something reserved for the early stages of a relationship.

Just because you're married doesn't mean dating is any less important. It's a way to keep both partners connected, igniting a spark of excitement and breaking up the monotony of family schedules. Dating allows you to shift from "mom" and "dad" to husband and wife.

When you invest in dating your spouse, you're saying, "You are worth the time and the monetary sacrifice." So, dress up and step out with the one you love. Genesis 2:24 instructs us to cleave to one another. Dating is the glue that helps keep your marriage strong.

DIFFER

A husband and wife can remain compatible even when they have differences. Agreeing to disagree is a valuable skill that allows a couple to stay united in direction while differing in opinion. Embracing diverse perspectives within a relationship can foster a deeper appreciation for each other's views.

Not seeing eye to eye on everything does not mean one is in opposition to the other. In the Bible, the concept of "reasoning together" is mentioned several times. This encourages discussing issues thoughtfully and with intellect, rather than emotion. A willingness to make concessions and listen to both sides helps a couple resolve differences by meeting each other halfway.

D

Activities

DEDICATION: "COUPLE'S TIME CAPSULE"

Activity: Create a "Couple's Time Capsule." Fill a box with items that symbolize your commitment—notes, photos, and mementos from meaningful moments. Set a date to open it in the future (e.g., 5 or 10 years) and write a dedication letter to include in the box.

Why It Inspires Growth: Building something tangible together celebrates your journey and future plans.

How It Builds Excitement: Anticipating the moment you'll open it keeps your dedication alive and adds a sense of adventure to your commitment.

DATING: "BLINDFOLD DATE NIGHT"

Activity: Plan a "Blindfold Date Night." Each spouse plans a surprise activity for the other but keeps it a secret until the moment arrives. Use a blindfold to heighten the suspense as you travel to each part of the date!

Why It Keeps Romance Alive: The mystery and surprise make even simple activities feel fresh and exciting.

How It Adds Fun: Laughing through the unexpected creates lighthearted memories you'll treasure together.

DIFFER: "SWITCH ROLES GAME"

Activity: Play the "Switch Roles Game." Each spouse pretends to be the other for a day! This includes trying to see things from their perspective and mimicking their decision-making process. Bonus points for humor!

Why It Fosters Understanding: Playfully stepping into each other's shoes encourages empathy and lightens serious differences.

How It Strengthens Teamwork: Finding humor in differences makes resolving them more collaborative and enjoyable.

E

EDIFY

Healthy couples are those who build each other up, not tear one another down. Edification should be noticed over time in a marriage. This is how a husband and wife can grow together, not apart. Improvement should be occurring over time as individuals and as a unit.

Encouraging growth mentally, spiritually, and physically should not be received as a threat or criticism when presented the right way. It should be part of your continued support for the other within the marriage. When you love your husband or wife, you should want them to become the best version of themselves. Knowledge puffs up, but love edifies (1 Corinthians 8:1)

ENDEARMENT

Terms of endearment are words of phrases that express love and affection. The only time a husband and wife should call each other out of their name is when they are calling them by cute, loving titles. Having a nick name or pet name is a way of individualizing your spouse.

It is also a public declaration of how you view their role in your life and how you feel about them, regardless of what is currently going on. 'Honey' refers to something sweet. 'Baby' is a paternal term, by reminds one of the love and care that should be expected. 'Sweetheart' expresses emotional closeness and fondness that is shown one to another.

God called David "the apple of His eye" (Psalm 17:8) as a term of endearment and it has permanently described his affection toward the king. When we call our spouse with endearment, we do the same.

EXCITEMENT

Keeping excitement within a marriage takes intentionality, especially if you have been together for a while. Planning for your future together, keeping short- term and long-term goals, and creating a culture that embraces new experiences are ways to ignite the fire of anticipation within the marriage. The bible says in Proverbs 5:18 that the husband is to rejoice with the wife of his youth.

This scripture instructs the couple that has been together for some time to remember what brought you both together and to celebrate their existence in one another's life. Purposely create moments of joy and pleasure to keep the thrill of your love alive.

E

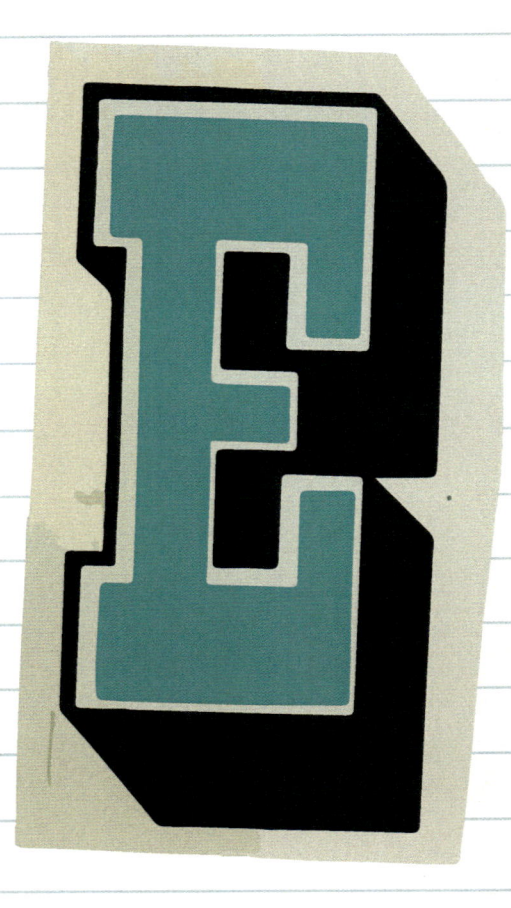

Activities

EDIFY: "COMPLIMENT CONTEST"

Activity: Host a "Compliment Contest." Take turns giving each other compliments, but the catch is to make each one more creative or heartfelt than the last. The first person to run out of ideas loses (and owes the other a treat!).

Why It Uplifts: Fun and genuine affirmations build each other up and strengthen your emotional bond.

How It Adds Playfulness: Turning compliments into a game keeps the mood light and joyful while fostering appreciation.

ENDEARMENT: "NICKNAMES JAR"

Activity: Create a "Nicknames Jar." Write down fun or affectionate nicknames for each other and draw one out daily to use throughout the day. Add a playful twist by making the other guess why you chose that name.

Why It Sparks Intimacy: Using endearing names creates a warm and loving atmosphere in your relationship.

How It Builds Connection: Sharing inside jokes and personal meanings behind names deepens your emotional closeness.

EXCITEMENT: "SPONTANEOUS ADVENTURE" CHALLENGE"

Activity: Try a "Spontaneous Adventure Challenge." Write down a list of fun activities (e.g., mini road trip, try a new food, dance in the living room) and pick one randomly to do on the spot.

Why It Boosts Energy: Breaking the routine and adding a sense of surprise keeps your relationship exciting.

How It Strengthens Joy: Experiencing something new together creates shared memories and a sense of adventure.

F

FAITHFUL

Remaining loyal and steadfast is easy when things are going smoothly. However, those qualities can be tested when faced with difficult times. Devotion should be threaded between the hearts of a husband and wife. When two hearts become knitted in faithfulness, loyalty is not easily swayed.

When a couple is faithful, they are reliable and committed to their relationship, during good times and bad. Proverbs 28:20 says a that a faithful man will abound in blessings. When a couple makes the decision to remain loyal to one another, they will both experience numerous blessings that will overflow from generation to generation.

FRIENDS

Friendship is vital in a healthy marriage. Mutual compatibility is the glue that keeps a couple fastened together. Friendship allows a safe space for honestly, vulnerability, and understanding. It also fosters mutual trust and support between husband and wife. Couples who use the label 'best friend' are those who keep their relationship first and foremost.

They enjoy spending time together and have a high value on creating memories. A husband who considers his wife a best friend will make sure she is the first to hear good or bad news. A wife who shares the same sentiment will make sure he is the first one she shares her day with. It's wonderful to know that the person you have given your heart to was created to love you at all times (Proverbs 17:17).

FORGIVENESS

A husband and wife who are quick to forgive each other are destined to stay together forever. Forgiveness is the ability to overlook faults and resolve offenses. This can happen by verbally asking for forgiveness when needed or it can be a decision that is made up in one's mind without the offense ever being addressed. Usually, it takes one offense to break down forgiveness within a marriage.

But, the bible gives us a number of times we are to forgive one person: 490 times (Matthew 18:21)! More than an apology, forgiveness is the willingness to move on without resentment. At times, this may take an increase of faith, but nothing is impossible. Just like God is always willing to forgive us for our wrong, a husband and wife should have the same loving ability. A marriage full of forgiveness is one that will thrive in love for one another and in the love of God.

F

Activities

FAITHFUL: "FAITH WALK TOGETHER"

Activity: Plan a "Faith Walk Together." Visit a scenic spot, such as a park or a hiking trail, and take a walk while sharing one way your faith has strengthened your relationship. End the walk with a short prayer or reflection together.

Why It Strengthens Bonds: Sharing your faith journey builds spiritual and emotional connection.

How It Brings Peace: Reflecting on your shared beliefs fosters unity and trust during life's challenges.

FRIENDS: "COUPLE'S GAME NIGHT"

Activity: Host a "Couple's Game Night." Invite your mutual friends over for an evening of fun games, snacks, and laughter. Play a couples-themed game where you answer questions about your relationship to see who knows each other best.

Why It Builds Camaraderie: Spending time with friends as a couple strengthens your social support network.

How It Creates Fun: Laughing together and sharing stories builds joyful memories with your friends and each other.

FORGIVENESS: "LET IT GO JAR"

Activity: Create a "Let It Go Jar." Write down any minor grievances or things that bothered you in the past week. Share them with your spouse, discuss them briefly, and then tear them up together to symbolize letting them go.

Why It Promotes Healing: Acknowledging and releasing small frustrations prevents resentment from building up.

How It Strengthens Trust: Demonstrating forgiveness shows your willingness to prioritize love over conflict.

G

GENTLE

Gentleness is a disposition and behavior that cultivates peace and harmony between a husband and a wife. When a couple remains mutually level-headed, especially during times of conflict, they can reason with logic and walk in wisdom. The volume of a voice should never be the determining factor of effectiveness.

A husband or wife can speak with confidence and clarity when they are committed to communicate with a quiet spirit and not a heavy hand. A couple who is quick to hear and slow to speak will be slow to anger when a culture of gentle coupling is embraced.

GRACIOUS

A gracious wife is one who is patient, understanding, and empathetic. She is willing to tolerate delays and handle disappointments believing that things always work out for the good. She can relate to her husband and his feelings by not just listening, but hearing what he has said.

Her sensitivity is a strength, not a weakness. Showing compassion to her husband affirms her connection to him and causes a greater bond to be formed. Proverbs 11:16 says that a gracious woman retains honor. A wife who is honored by her husband is a living example of grace.

GENEROUS

When a husband shows a readiness to give more than what is expected, he is generous. It's more than showing kindness. It is the willingness to self-sacrifice. Giving to your wife is more than monetarily. It is giving her time and attention. When he completely trusts the cause of his role, he will not struggle with selfishness.

Being kindhearted comes easy to a man who is leaning into the goodness of God. Proverbs 11:25 says that a generous person will prosper; whoever refreshes will be refreshed. A husband's generosity will cause his wife to strengthen him as he strengthens her with his unselfish love.

G

Activities

GENTLE: "GENTLE WORDS ONLY DAY"

Activity: Have a "Gentle Words Only Day." Commit to speaking only kind, affirming, and encouraging words to each other for an entire day. Bonus: Write down a few of the gentlest things your spouse says and share how they made you feel at the end of the day.

Why It Creates Calm: Gentle communication fosters a peaceful and loving atmosphere in your relationship.

How It Deepens Intimacy: Prioritizing tenderness helps you focus on each other's emotional needs.

GRACIOUS: "GRATITUDE CHALLENGE"

Activity: Play the "Gratitude Challenge." Each spouse lists three things they are grateful for about the other—big or small. Share your lists and take turns explaining why those actions or qualities meant so much to you.

Why It Encourages Positivity: Focusing on gratitude highlights the good in your relationship and strengthens emotional bonds.

How It Builds Appreciation: Recognizing each other's efforts fosters mutual respect and love.

GENEROUS: "SPOIL YOUR SPOUSE DAY"

Activity: Create a "Spoil Your Spouse Day." Dedicate the day to being intentionally generous toward your spouse. Prepare their favorite meal, offer to do a task they dislike, or surprise them with something small but meaningful, like a love note or a thoughtful gift.

Why It Strengthens Connection: Acts of generosity show your spouse they are valued and cherished.

How It Builds Joy: Thoughtful gestures foster happiness and create positive memories within your relationship.

H

HEALTH

A healthy marriage is not a perfect marriage. It is a union that is free from injury or illness. In every relationship, there are times when feelings of pain, discomfort, distress, or weakness need to be managed. When a husband and wife are willing to work together to heal and maintain health within the marriage, they will not succumb to the damage that has been caused.

Deciding to quickly resolve issues, regularly having honest conversations, and diligently remaining concerned about one another's well-being, are ways to alleviate the possibility of long-term effects of hurt feelings. Jeremiah 33:6 says "…I will bring health and healing; I will heal them and reveal to them the abundance of peace and truth." A healthy marriage will be one full of peace because the husband and wife are not afraid to face the truth by having conversations that heal, not hurt.

HONOR

A husband feels loved when he is honored. A wife that shows him high respect and great esteem is a woman who is admires him. She has confidence in his ability and celebrates his achievements. Her husband's feelings and views are valued, although not necessarily agreed with.

She gives the same consideration that she would expect from him. The reason why it is easy to honor him is because she shows herself honor. She is proud to be married to him and grateful to be his wife. Ephesians 5:33 instructs the wife to "…respect her husband." When a wife feels loved, it is easy for her to honor her husband.

HARD CONVERSATIONS

Sitting down together and discussing obvious issues between a husband and wife is considered a hard conversation. It is when a moment of time is carved out to rationally talk about the problem with an intent to solve it. Acknowledging that there is an issue should not be seen as a threat to the husband if he is the one causing the problem.

Likewise, the wife should not feel attacked if she is the one who needs to be confronted. Announcing that a hard conversation is needed is a way to forewarn one another. Proverbs 15 explains that "…a gentle answer turns away wrath, but a harsh word stirs up anger." When you approach issues with wise words and spirit-led communication, you are more likely to put out a fire instead of adding fuel to it.

H

Activities

HEALTH: "WELLNESS DAY TOGETHER"

Activity: Plan a "Wellness Day Together." Choose an activity that promotes health, like cooking a nutritious meal, going for a long walk, or taking a yoga class together. End the day by setting one small health goal to support each other with.

Why It Builds Well-Being: Prioritizing health as a couple strengthens physical and emotional connection.

How It Encourages Teamwork: Supporting each other's wellness goals fosters accountability and mutual care.

HONOR: "TRIBUTE TIME CAPSULE"

Activity: Create a "Tribute Time Capsule." Write a heartfelt note honoring your spouse's qualities, accomplishments, or efforts that you deeply admire. Seal it in an envelope for them to open on a future date, like an anniversary or birthday.

Why It Uplifts: Honoring your spouse's strengths reinforces their sense of worth and your admiration.

How It Fosters Connection: Intentional words of honor strengthen respect and deepen emotional intimacy.

HARD CONVERSATIONS: "COFFEE TABLE TALK"

Activity: Try the "Coffee Table Talk." Schedule a dedicated time to discuss a tough topic in a calm and neutral setting, like over coffee. Set ground rules: no interruptions, active listening, and focus on solutions rather than blame.

Why It Promotes Understanding: Creating a safe space for dialogue reduces tension and encourages honesty.

How It Builds Trust: Handling hard conversations respectfully reinforces your ability to navigate challenges together.

i

INTEREST

A married couple has a lower chance of growing apart if they do the following: share the same interests and respect the unshared interests. Although the husband and wife are seen as one in the sight of God, they are still individuals. Sharing the same tastes in entertainment, engaging in the same hobbies, and spending leisure time together are important. But, having a dislike for a particular past-time the husband or wife enjoys should not cause the other to feel annoyed. A wife should be able to appreciate her husband's intrigue about something she is not fond of. A husband, also, should be willing to support his wife's attraction to something he doesn't care for. There should also be moments when compromise plays a part, and the husband or wife gives in to what the other enjoys with an attempt to understand what is so appealing. Amos 3:3 says "…how can two walk together unless they agree." You can continue to walk together in your marriage while not always doing the same things together.

INTIMACY

Intimacy is more than a husband and wife making love. Although sexual health is vital to a marriage, so it the ability to share vulnerable moments, difficult details, and emotional episodes with one another. A husband who can talk to his wife about personal challenges he may be having, and a wife who feels comfortable describing how she truly feels is like standing naked and unafraid in front of one another. Praying together is another form of intimacy.

During those moments, requests are being made to God while also admitting each desperate need for Him to be involved in their lives. The goodness of God is expressed when the marital duty is fulfilled in the bedroom. It is also removes shame and opens up opportunities for a couple to enjoy the greatest intimacy of all; a dual closeness with the Lord.

INTEGRITY

Marriage vows are made with integrity. No matter if made in the church house or the courthouse, an honest moment was created in front of spiritual or legal authority with witnesses. Each were asked to honestly profess their love and commitment to one another with a refusal to change.

A pledge was made to remain responsible, trustworthy, and responsible until death do you part. But integrity only works when the husband and wife chose to do the right thing for the sake of the marriage, and not just for themselves. If the husband or wife breaks a wedding vow but is willing to repair it, he or she is being integral. Mark 10:9 "…what God has joined together, let no man separate." When integrity is upheld, even after a mishap, the husband and wife will refuse to separate from one another.

i

Activities

INTEREST: "SHARED HOBBY DAY"

Activity: Plan a "Shared Hobby Day." Pick an activity that interests both of you or something new you've always wanted to try, like cooking a unique recipe, learning a dance move, or exploring a local attraction. Dedicate the day to diving into it together.

Why It Builds Connection: Sharing interests strengthens your bond and creates fun, meaningful memories.

How It Sparks Joy: Exploring something new together keeps your relationship fresh and exciting.

INTIMACY: "MEMORY LANE MOMENTS"

Activity: Play "Memory Lane Moments." Each partner picks one special memory from your relationship to recount in detail. Share how that moment made you feel and why it strengthened your love.

Why It Deepens Bonding: Reliving cherished memories rekindles emotional and physical closeness.

How It Fosters Intimacy: Reflecting on your journey brings gratitude for the love you've built together.

INTEGRITY: "PROMISE BOARD"

Activity: Create a "Promise Board." Write down individual and shared commitments to your relationship, such as keeping your word, being honest, or prioritizing each other's well-being. Display it as a reminder of your values.

Why It Strengthens Trust: Clear, visible promises reinforce accountability and reliability.

How It Builds Respect: Living with integrity fosters admiration and confidence in your partnership.

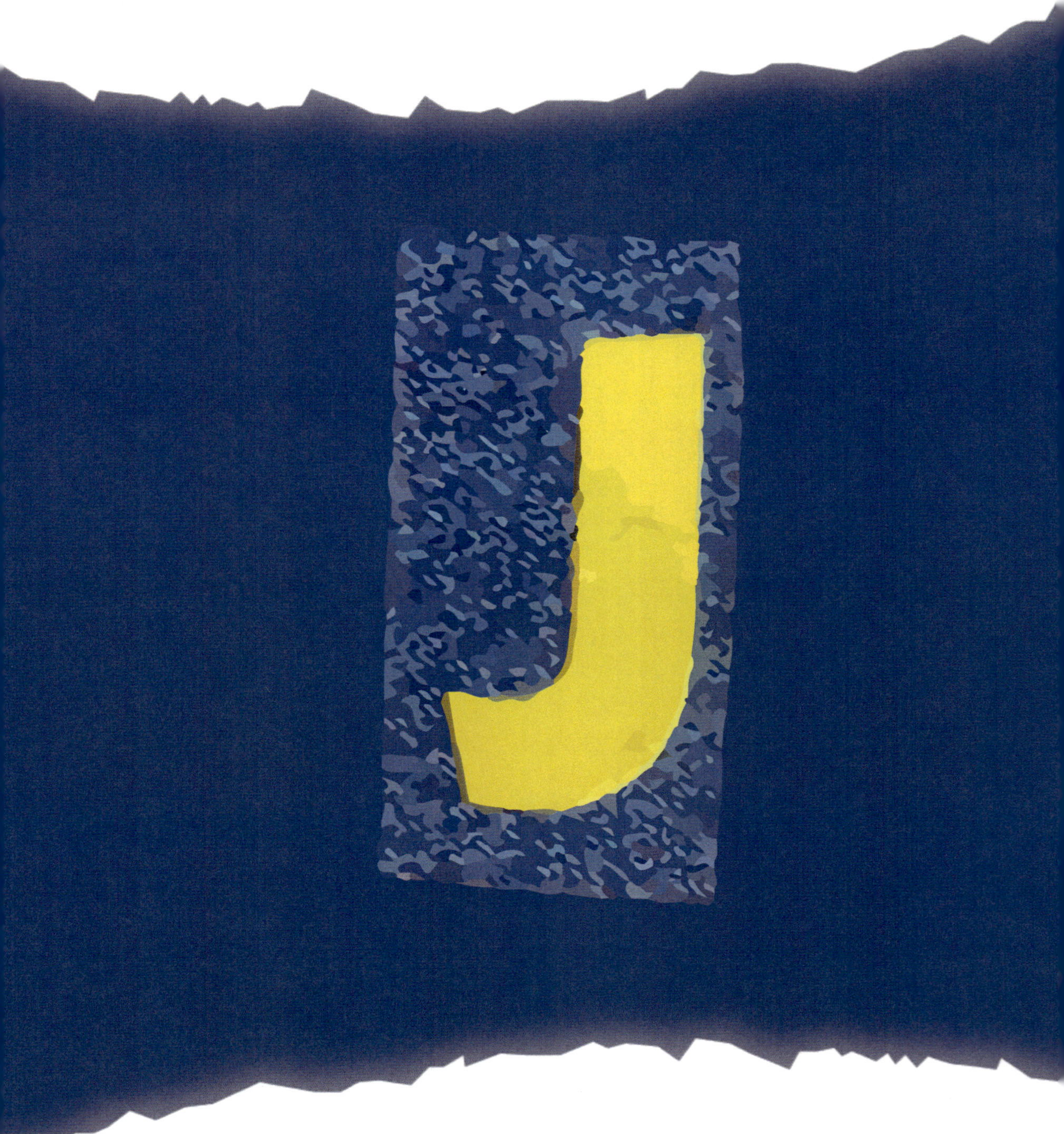
J

JEALOUSY

The true definition of jealousy is the fear of being replaced. A wife who struggles with jealousy is most likely feeling this fear. She is anticipating abandonment from her husband. A husband who struggles with this negative emotion is most likely feeling the same way. The way to remedy this within a marriage is to admit how you are feeling and then discover why. Maybe it's a new baby in the house that is getting all the wife's attention. Perhaps the husband is getting older and not feeling his best physically. Could it be the wife is realizing her once flawless skin is giving in to frown and laugh lines. Maybe the husband is not as far in his career as he thought he would be and doubts his ability to care for his family. There are countless reasons that could be at the root of jealousy. Whatever the reason, it needs to be tamed. Proverbs 27:4 says "Anger is cruel, and wrath is like a flood, but jealousy is even more dangerous." Feeling jealous in a marriage without a resolve could possibly cause unrepairable damage.

JADED

A wife or husband who has been jaded within the marriage is one who lacks enthusiasm due to dealing with too much of something. Repeated disappointments, continued mistakes, and lack of consideration are some examples that causes deterioration. If a husband or wife who has been difficult or continues bad behavior will eventually give up because of fatigue. He or she will begin with withdraw from the marriage and ignore the patterns that have caused the break down. Lack of concern means that no more effort will be made to repair the breach. The only remedy to stop feeling jaded is forgiveness. Because a pattern caused the destruction, a new pattern must be implemented. Asking for forgiveness or deciding to forgive stops the cycle and clears the way for a new start. Colossians 3:13 instructs us to, "bear with one another, and if one has a complaint against another, forgiving each other, as the Lord has forgiven you, so you must forgive." Jesus has created a weapon against feeling jaded by providing us the ability to forgive, as He has forgiven us.

JABBING

The method of jabbing is one created by boxers to keep their opponent at a distance. It is a type of defense. When a wife or husband continues to jab their loved with hurtful words, criticism, sarcasm, or reminders of mistakes is keeps the couple at a distance. A husband or wife who negatively nudges see each other as enemies. Verbal abuse can be worse than physical abuse at times. Ephesians 4:29-32 says to not let unwholesome talk come out of your mouths, but only what is helpful for building others up according to their needs that it may benefit those who listen. Instead of talking down to one another, speak words that uplift. When a husband and wife make the decision to take the gloves off and stop being sparring partners, they will begin to build each other up instead of beat each other up.

J

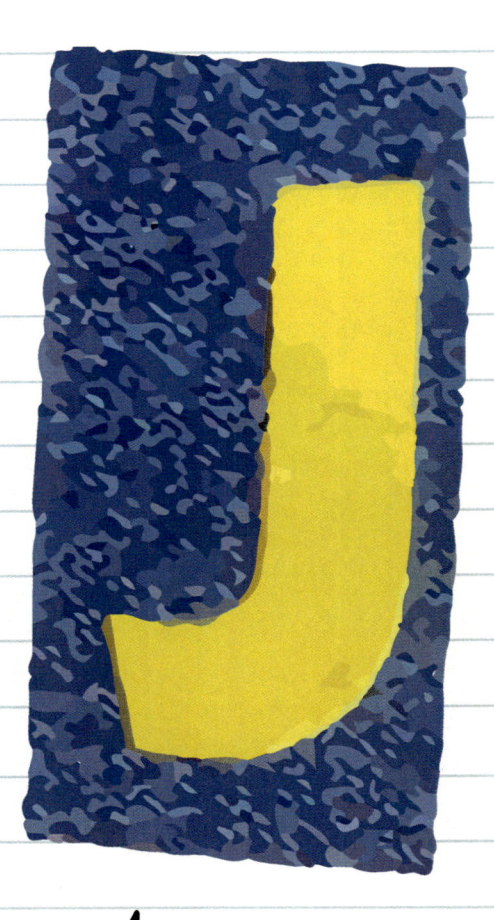

Activities

JEALOUSY: "REASSURANCE RITUAL"

Activity: Try the "Reassurance Ritual." When feelings of jealousy arise, take turns sharing one insecurity and one thing your partner does to make you feel secure. Then, affirm each other with a specific compliment or reassurance that addresses the insecurity.

Why It Promotes Understanding: Addressing jealousy openly reduces its impact and fosters trust.

How It Builds Security: Offering reassurance helps both partners feel valued and safe in the relationship.

JADED: "GRATITUDE RESET"

Activity: Plan a "Gratitude Reset." Create a list of three things you appreciate about your relationship and three ways you'd like to reignite excitement (e.g., planning a getaway, trying something new together). Share your lists and choose one idea to act on immediately.

Why It Rekindles Excitement: Focusing on gratitude and shared goals shifts your perspective and reduces feelings of disillusionment.

How It Revives Energy: Taking action on fun ideas brings joy and renewal to your partnership.

JABBING: "PAUSE AND PRAISE GAME"

Activity: Practice the "Pause and Praise Game." When you catch yourself or your spouse making a sharp remark, pause, and instead, replace it with a compliment or positive statement. Keep score to see who catches themselves more often!

Why It Reduces Conflict: Replacing negativity with praise diffuses tension and encourages kindness.

How It Builds Positivity: Redirecting energy toward affirmations fosters a more uplifting and supportive dynamic.

K

KINDNESS

Kindness in a marriage is one that is caring and helpful. A husband who is willing to assist his wife, with or without asking, expresses understanding and grace. A wife who is kind is generous to her husband with her time and shows concern for him. Compassion is what keeps kindness unconditional.

A husband and wife who remain caring, no matter what is currently going on between them, have mastered the art of true kindness. They no longer allow their differences to stop them from being benevolent. They can overlook how they feel and work hard to maintain a relationship that is considerate.

1 Corinthians 13:1 "Love is patient and kind…". True love is consistently kind.

KEEP

A common phrase recited in wedding vows is 'to have and to hold'. In other words, a vow has been made between the husband and wife to keep one another. A wife who is being kept is one who is being enjoyed, preserved, and maintained by her husband. A husband who is being kept is one who is supported, helped, and protected by his wife's love.

This couple does not want to throw away the marriage. They are working hard not to lose it. They are both determined to continue growing as a married couple and exclusively belong to each other. Romans 12:9 "Love must be sincere. Hate what is evil, cling to what is good." A kept husband and wife are individuals who are holding on by the grace of God.

KNOWLEDGE

Because people change, you must expect your husband or wife to change. After the 3-6 months that is said to get to know each other while dating, the continued effort to explore their life should never stop. The more you know your husband or wife, and how they have evolved over the years, the less you could fall into the idea of who think you married instead of the reality of who they are.

Spending quality time together, talking about personal goals, or discussing current social issues are ways to keep the deep dive going. Flirting, actively listening, and laughing together is another way to continue researching your spouse. Only God knows who we really are because He has created our lives and watches over our evolution. Jeremiah 1:5 says, "before I formed you in the womb, I knew you…". Because of this truth, it is vital that the husband and wife never grow weary of getting to know each other as each develops over time.

K

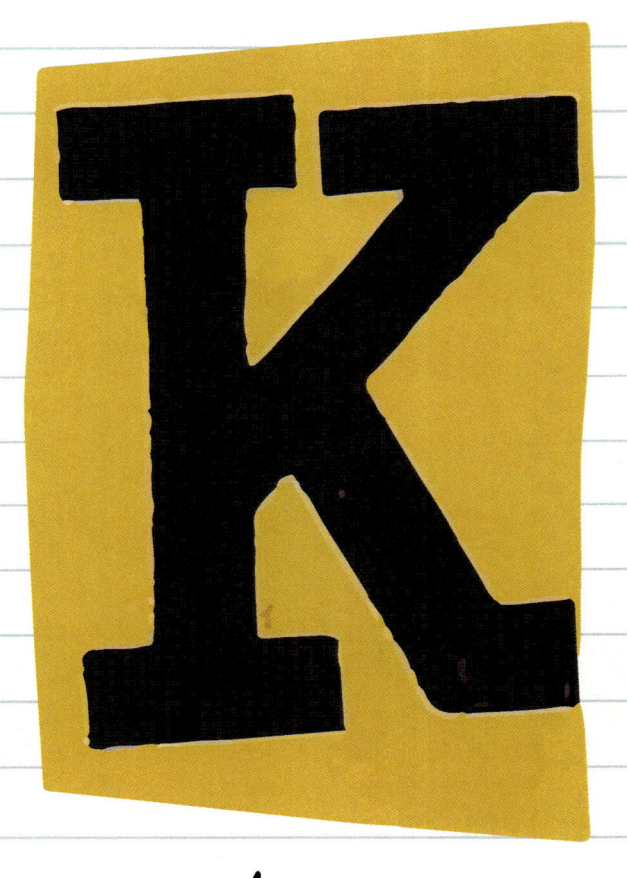

Activities

KINDNESS: "KINDNESS SCAVENGER HUNT"

Activity: Plan a "Kindness Scavenger Hunt." Write small notes of encouragement, compliments, or acts of love, and hide them in places your spouse will find throughout the week (e.g., their bag, car, or on their pillow). End the week by sharing which note or act meant the most to each of you.

Why It Fosters Love: Unexpected moments of kindness create excitement and warmth in your relationship.

How It Builds Connection: Thoughtful gestures remind your spouse that they are cherished and appreciated daily.

KEEP: "RELATIONSHIP SCRAPBOOK"

Activity: Design a "Relationship Scrapbook." Dedicate an evening to start a scrapbook together, including photos, ticket stubs, notes, or drawings that represent special moments. Add a few pages each month and take time to revisit it on anniversaries or special occasions.

Why It Creates Nostalgia: Capturing milestones in a creative way allows you to relive cherished memories.

How It Strengthens Partnership: Working on a shared project encourages teamwork and celebrates the growth of your relationship.

KNOWLEDGE: "TEACH ME SOMETHING NIGHT"

Activity: Have a "Teach Me Something Night." Each partner chooses a skill, recipe, or piece of knowledge to share with the other—something you're good at or passionate about. Take turns teaching and learning from each other.

Why It Inspires Growth: Learning together keeps the relationship dynamic and engaging.

How It Builds Connection: Sharing knowledge fosters mutual respect and creates fun, memorable experiences.

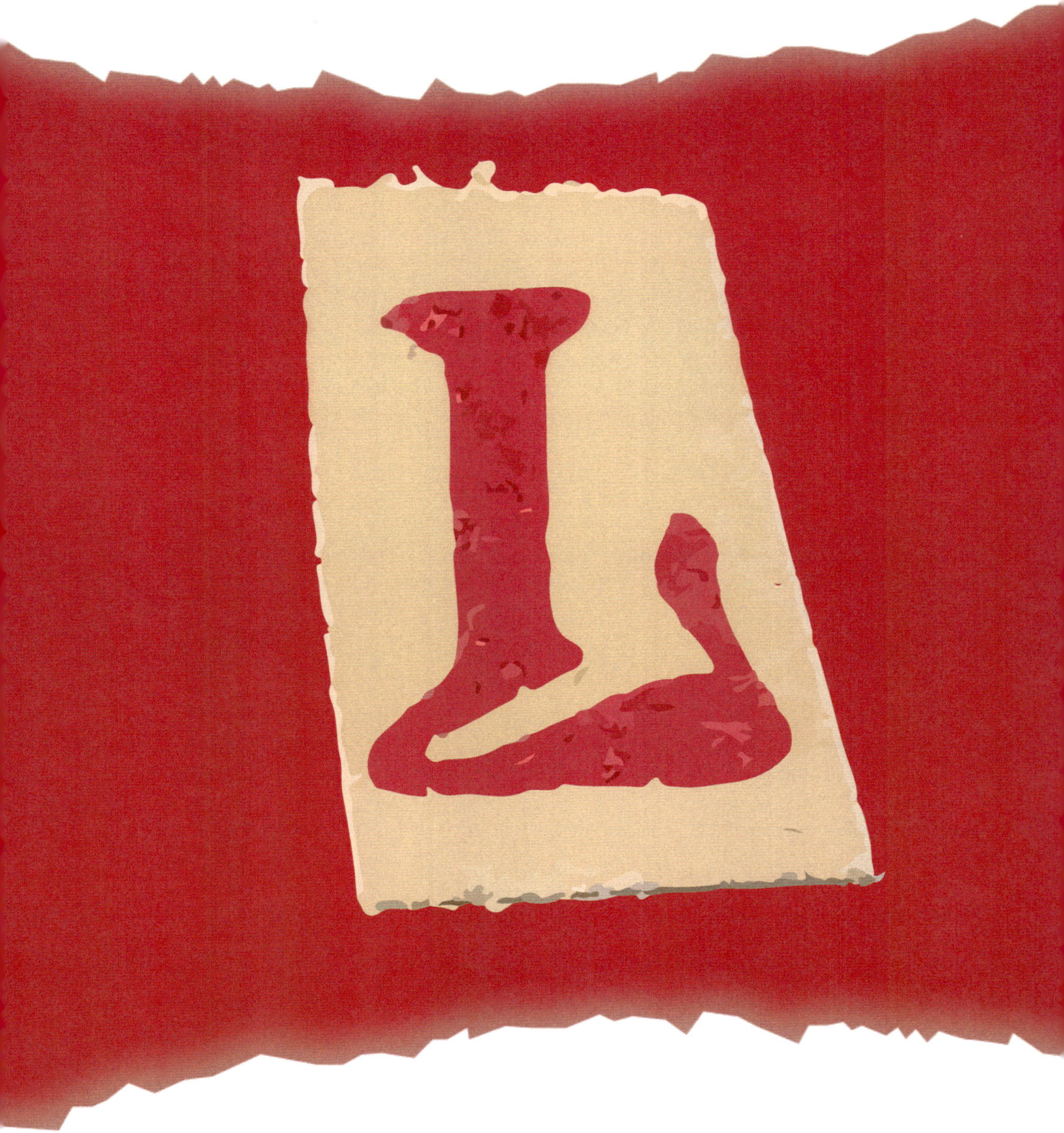
L

LOVE

A husband who loves his wife has deep affection for her. A wife who loves her husband is attached to him. Their devotion is felt by others and can be seen by all who pay attention. A bond is created between the two of them that creates a sense of closeness and commitment.

Love is what burns the fire of passion and desire. But love is more than a feeling. The bible says that it is "patient, kind; it does not boast, it is not proud. It does not dishonor others, it is not selfish, it is not easily angered, it keeps no records of wrongs. Love does not delight in evil but rejoices with the truth. It (love) always protects, always trusts, always hopes, always preserves. Love never fails." 1 Corinthians 13:4-8 A marriage full of love will not fail.

LISTEN

A wife who listens is one who gives her attention to not just his voice, but his mannerisms. She can not only discern the tone, but in some cases, translate what he really trying to say. She understands that the first step to communication is effectively hearing what is being said with awareness and understanding. Her husband knows that she can pull out subtexts that may be hidden behind words that are being used. He knows that she will connect the dots and even paraphrase to make sure what she heard is correct. A husband who is listened to should extend the same courtesy to her.

James 1:19 says that everyone should be quick to listen, slow to speak and slow to become angry. When a husband and wife cannot just listen, but hear what is being said, the less they will become angry with one another.

LEAD

A husband who leads his house is a man who is ready and willing to guide his wife in a certain way. He can positively influence her by living a life of strength and direction. Usually, a wife is willing to follow her husband if he is clear and consistent with his leadership. The bible is clear in Ephesians 5:22 "Wives, follow the lead of your own husbands as you follow the Lord."

Wife, just as you follow Christ you are to follow your husband. If you are the follower, he is the leader. The only way this system works is when the wife is willing to be the follower and allow the husband to be the leader. Following can be hard. It takes trust and that may need to be built with opportunity and time. Allow your husband to take his rightful place in the home as the leader of his family. Your part in the marriage is just as significant, although it may not be first.

L

Activities

LOVE: "HEARTFELT PLAYLIST"

Activity: Create a "Heartfelt Playlist." Each partner picks songs that remind them of the other or reflect their love story. Spend an evening listening to the playlist together and sharing the reasons behind your choices.

Why It Sparks Emotion: Music has the power to evoke deep feelings and create meaningful memories.

How It Strengthens Bonding: Sharing personal thoughts through songs fosters vulnerability and connection.

LISTEN: "QUESTION ROULETTE"

Activity: Play "Question Roulette." Write down thoughtful or fun questions about your relationship or dreams on slips of paper and place them in a bowl. Take turns drawing and answering while the other actively listens and asks follow-up questions.

Why It Builds Understanding: Thoughtful questions encourage meaningful dialogue and attentiveness.

How It Deepens Respect: Actively listening to each other's answers shows care and interest in their thoughts and feelings.

LEAD: "FUTURE GOALS ADVENTURE MAP"

Activity: Plan a "Future Goals Adventure Map." Use a large sheet of paper to draw a map of your future together. Include milestones like trips, personal goals, or relationship aspirations, and plot the path to each one. Hang it where you can see it often and update it as you go.

Why It Inspires Motivation: Visualizing your future goals keeps you focused and aligned as a team.

How It Encourages Collaboration: Creating a shared vision promotes teamwork and excitement about your journey together.

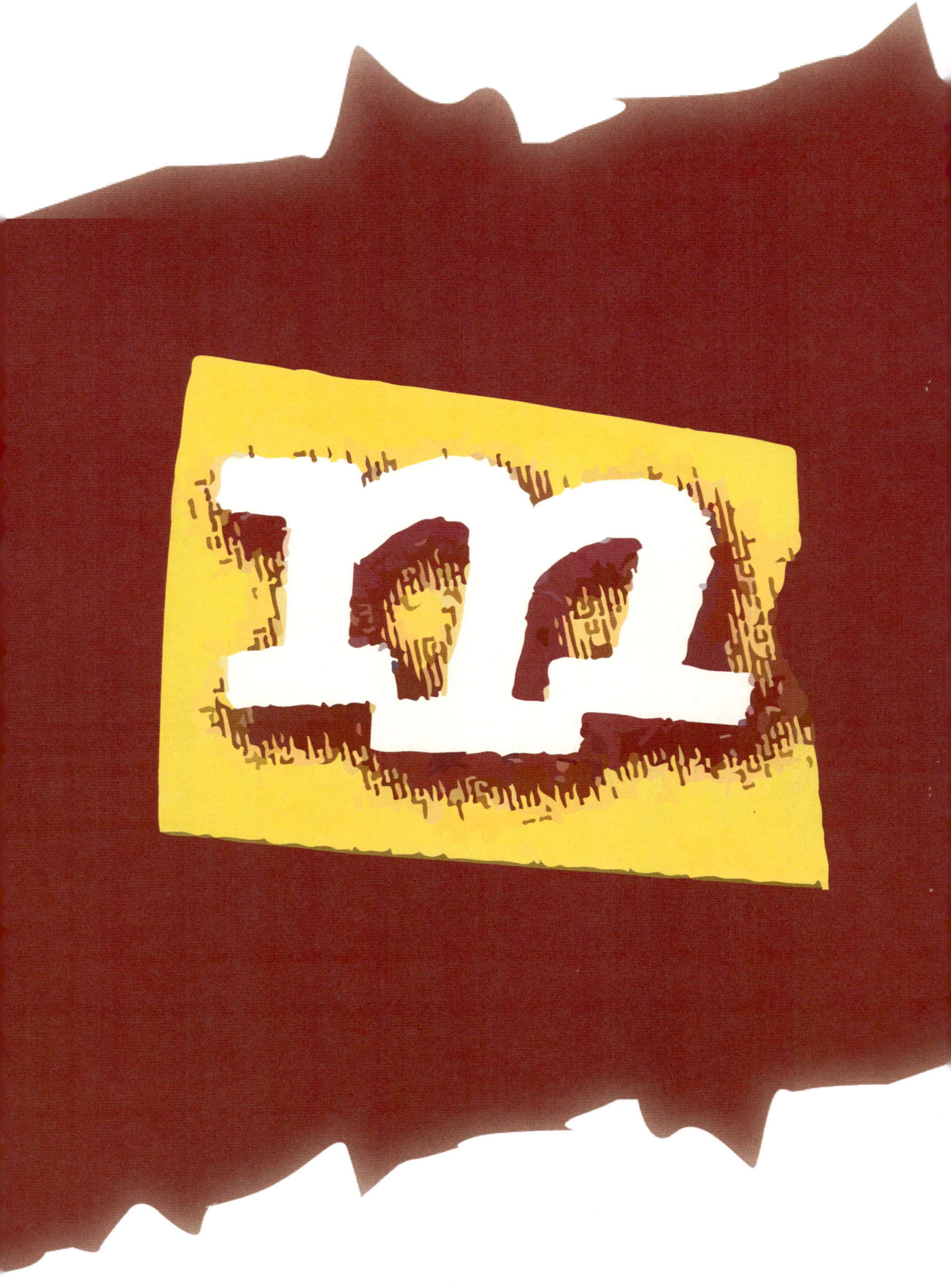
m

MOTIVATE

A wife who motivates her husband is one who stimulates him to act in a certain manner. She can encourage him to become the best version of himself. She is persistent in her belief in his abilities and is intensely committed to his process. Her words are full of inspiration and stimulation.

When he shares an idea, she is ready and willing to boost his proposal with creative strategies and realistic timelines. She is a compliment to his complex mind. Her motivation doesn't distract him, it reinforces. Genesis 2:18 says "it is not good for man to be alone. I will make him a help mate (a partner) for him." The ability to motivate should be natural for the wife who embraces her role and believes in her husband.

MEND

A husband and wife who are willing to admit something within the marriage has been damaged and are willing to do the work to repair it, is a couple who doesn't mind the mending. Repairing a relationship takes continuous effort and die-hard dedication. Apologizing acknowledges the offense, but empathizing personalizes it. When a couple can understand and share the feelings about how it made them feel, they have sympathy for one another.

This will cause connection and compassion while the two are working on restoring their relationship. Mending a marriage takes time and patience. It takes a willingness to move forward and the discipline to not look back. Ultimately, the Lord is the only One who can restore. 1 Peter 5:10 "…the Lord himself with restore you, make you firm, and steadfast." Once He has done the mending, your marriage will become solid and unwavering.

MINDFUL

A mindful marriage is one that is concerned about what is currently happening versus what has happened in the past. A husband and wife who are insightful and open minded see their marriage with clarity without preconceived ideas. Building a life together this way allows the husband and wife to live without jumping to conclusions. It also helps the couple to remain forward focused, keeping them both on the path to happily-ever-after.

A wife who is mindful avoids destructive responses and habits while a husband who is in the same state of mind does the same. They both have learned to observe thoughts, emotions, and present-moment experiences without reacting to them. Romans 12:2 "…be transformed by the renewal of your mind." A couple who have renewed their mind will be transformed into the power couple they were always meant to be.

Activities

MOTIVATE: "GOAL CHALLENGE"

Activity: Start a "Goal Challenge." Each partner sets one personal or shared goal for the week, and you check in daily to encourage and motivate each other. End the week by celebrating the progress with a fun reward, like a dinner date or a movie night.

Why It Drives Progress: Encouragement and accountability create momentum toward achieving goals.

How It Builds Support: Cheering each other on strengthens trust and partnership.

MEND: "RENEWAL DINNER"

Activity: Host a "Renewal Dinner." Cook or order a meal together, then use the time to share one thing you appreciate about each other and one area where you'd like to grow as a couple. End the dinner by toasting to your commitment to move forward positively.

Why It Restores Harmony: Creating a warm, intentional space makes tough conversations feel less daunting.

How It Strengthens Connection: Reflecting on growth and showing vulnerability fosters trust and unity.

MINDFUL: "MINDFUL MOMENT EXCHANGE"

Activity: Try a "Mindful Moment Exchange." Each partner picks a simple daily activity (like having coffee or folding laundry) and makes it special by focusing entirely on the moment together—no phones, no distractions, just presence.

Why It Creates Calm: Mindful attention to small moments helps you appreciate the here and now.

How It Builds Intimacy: Sharing uninterrupted, intentional time fosters closeness and gratitude.

N

NEEDS

A husband and wife who are meeting each other's needs are a couple who has prioritized fulfilling basic requirements to live a loving life. Needs are required in a marriage to cultivate a safe, healthy, and loving atmosphere. Meeting those needs are vital to the survival of the relationship.

If the wife needs time to feel loved, the husband should freely give her what she wants. If the husband needs affection to feel love, the wife should also give him what he desires. Fulfilling needs within a marriage is a selfless act of service.

God is always willing to fulfill all of our needs (Philippians 4:19) and a husband and wife should be willing to do the same for one another.

NOTICE

When a wife is noticed by her husband, she feels admired. It means that he took time to look at her with love and approval. When a wife can notice that her husband is missing something, and she provides it, he feels she is thoughtful and reliable. Taking notice in a marriage is proof that there is a common feeling; that feeling is concern.

Noticing means to take interest and pay attention to someone. When you are noticed by your spouse, it will make you feel seen. The eyes of the Lord are attentive to those who belong to Him (1 Peter 3:12). The eyes of the husband and wife should also remain attentive.

NICE

Sometimes the best way to improve your marriage is by being nice.
A couple who compliments each other, who are lovingly honest, and who show an interest in how they are feeling would be considered a couple who are just plain nice.

Being around a wife who is pleasant allows a husband to feel comfortable and at ease. Having a husband who is friendly and treats others well allows the wife to feel confident at home and in public settings.

More than being generous with acts of kindness, a nice spouse is generous with joy. Being nice is when you can bear all things, believe all things, hope for all things and endure all things in love (1 Corinthians 13:7).

N

Activities

NEEDS: "NEEDS CHECK-IN"

Activity: Try a "Needs Check-In." Set aside 15 minutes to ask each other, "What do you need more of from me this week?" and "What can I do to help?" Write down the answers and make a plan to fulfill at least one of those needs together.

Why It Enhances Understanding: Proactively addressing each other's needs reduces misunderstandings.

How It Builds Support: Showing care for each other's well-being strengthens trust and partnership.

NOTICE: "NOTICE SOMETHING NEW GAME"

Activity: Play the "Notice Something New Game." Spend a day intentionally observing your spouse's habits, actions, or appearance. At the end of the day, share one new thing you noticed that you admire or appreciate.

Why It Creates Awareness: Paying attention reminds you to value the small things often overlooked.

How It Strengthens Appreciation: Highlighting unnoticed details fosters gratitude and emotional closeness.

NICE: "KINDNESS RELAY"

Activity: Plan a "Kindness Relay." Take turns doing something nice for each other throughout the day, like making breakfast, sending a sweet text, or completing a small task for the other. See how many nice things you can exchange!

Why It Spreads Joy: Acts of kindness create a ripple effect of positivity in your relationship.

How It Builds Affection: Small, thoughtful gestures remind your spouse of your care and thoughtfulness.

0

OPTIMISTIC

Optimism is having hope for the future. Couple gets married to end up divorced. It is a union that starts with confidence that it will last forever. But hope can fade over the years from the typical wear and tear ever marriage endures. But if a husband or wife has the wherewithal to continue to think good things will happen and remains hopeful of it despite of what it may look like, hope can be resuscitated. Expectation has a way to supernaturally breathe life back into what may seem like a hopeless situation.

Optimism is a strength and is an example of steadfastness. It has a way of supernaturally giving you strength, especially during difficult times. Romans 12:12 Rejoice in hope, be patient in tribulation, be constant in prayer. Optimism in the marriage can cause a couple to celebrate what could be, no matter what may currently be going on.

OWNERSHIP

Ownership is being accountable for your own actions and results. When a husband and wife decide to take initiative and admit their shortcomings, this is a couple who will not only survive but thrive. Ownership also cultivates problem solving between the two and destroys the blame game. It is a way to resolve issues quickly and efficiently. Taking responsibility is a sure-fire way to take charge in life because the husband or wife are not being secretive or selective on how their actions will affect one another.

Proverbs 28:13 says "whoever conceals his transgression will not prosper, but he who confesses and forsakes them will obtain mercy." A husband and wife who are quick to own mistakes are sure to receive what they may not deserve; mercy.

OBLIGATION

Marriage causes the husband and wife to be obligated to one another. Although the word 'obligation' can come across as a negative one, because something might be done out of duty and not desire, it still produces positive results between the husband and wife. The truth is, the husband and wife both owe each other love, commitment, and dedication because of the formal contract they made on their marriage day.

They are both responsible for fulfilling said obligation, even when it may feel like a burden. Romans 13:7 says pay all what is owed…respect to whom respect is owed, honor to whom honor is owed. Obligation can be seen as a debt that was accompanied with the marriage certificate. And that debt, no matter how old, will never be paid until death do you part.

0

Activities

OPTIMISTIC: "POSITIVE VISION NIGHT"

Activity: Host a "Positive Vision Night." Sit down together and share your hopes and dreams for the future, focusing on what excites you about your relationship. Write down one optimistic goal for the next month and plan how to work toward it as a team.

Why It Inspires Growth: Focusing on a bright future reinforces hope and strengthens your bond.

How It Builds Confidence: Shared optimism fuels motivation and emotional connection.

OWNERSHIP: "OWNERSHIP REFLECTION NIGHT"

Activity: Plan a "Ownership Reflection Night." Each partner shares one area of the relationship or household they feel responsible for and take pride in managing. Discuss ways to support each other in those roles and celebrate the contributions made.

Why It Encourages Accountability: Reflecting on responsibilities reinforces a sense of purpose and commitment.

How It Builds Collaboration: Recognizing and supporting each other's efforts strengthens teamwork and mutual respect.

OBLIGATION: "RE-FRAME THE ROUTINE DAY"

Activity: Plan a "Re-frame the Routine Day." Turn an everyday obligation (like cooking dinner or running errands) into an opportunity to connect. Do the task together and make it fun by adding music, playful competition, or sharing stories while you work.

Why It Changes Perspective: Turning obligations into bonding moments fosters joy in the mundane.

How It Strengthens Partnership: Collaborating on daily tasks reinforces teamwork and shared purpose.

P

PEACE

The most peaceful place in the world should be the married couple's home. More than shelter, it should be a dwelling that is calm and free from disturbances. The husband will want to come home after work because he knows there is a quietness that he can only find in his residence. This quietness doesn't have anything to do with the level of noise, it is all about the environment. The wife should ensure that tranquility fills the atmosphere not for his peace, but for hers as well. She should enjoy the fact that her husband can find rest in the home she has created for him. The halls are not filled with hostility. The rooms are not cluttered and chaotic. There is a feeling of wholeness saturated in the home. Isaiah 32:18 says, "Then my people will dwell in a peaceful place, in safe and secure homes, in undisturbed places of rest."

PASSION

A passionate marriage is fueled by a very powerful sexual desire. Most married couples start with this being one of the key components to their decision to tie the knot. But over time, the passion can feel like it is dying or could die altogether. Excluding normal seasons of life, (i.e. children, illness, physical challenges, crisis, growing old, etc.) passion should still flow between the husband and wife. Intentionally creating time for love making is a way to ensure intimate moments are regularly occurring. Looking at one another with desire and giving into that desire is another way to add a spark to the flame. Wearing something sexy to bed, or nothing at all, is another way to ignite the fire again. Hebrews13:4 says that marriage is to be honored by all and the marriage bed is undefiled. Whatever happens in your marriage bed is blessed by God and is looked upon as holy. Understanding this will give a husband and wife purpose for their passion.

PATIENCE

Patience is the ability to wait. It is when a husband and wife can do something, despite difficulty, without complaining. There are situations in a marriage that can only be rectified with patience. Learning interpersonal skills, managing schedules, and simply going through trials and tribulations are moments where patience is an absolute necessity the husband and wife must have. Sometimes a couple is faced with challenges that purposely cause them to slow down. Other times it may be a time of testing and resolve within their marriage. Whatever the reason is, patience is developed only by encountering moments that cause you to remain patient. It takes faith, strength, and time. Ecclesiastes 7:8 says, "Better is the end of a thing than its beginning, and the patient in spirit is better than the proud in spirit." God's word promises that if you are willing to wait with patience for whatever you are waiting for, it will be better in the end.

P

Activities

PEACE: "CALM TOGETHER RITUAL"

Activity: Create a "Calm Together Ritual." Choose an activity that brings both of you peace, like meditating, listening to calming music, or taking a quiet walk. Do this together once a week to center yourselves and reconnect.

Why It Fosters Harmony: Shared moments of calm reduce stress and enhance emotional balance.

How It Builds Connection: Relaxing together strengthens the bond and reinforces a sense of safety.

PASSION: "DREAM DATE NIGHT IN"

Activity: Plan a "Dream Date Night In." Recreate a romantic setting at home with candles, music, and a special dinner. Take turns sharing one thing you're most passionate about in life or in your relationship, and reflect on how it fuels your connection.

Why It Rekindles Fire: Passionate moments remind you of the spark that brought you together.

How It Deepens Intimacy: Sharing what drives you creates emotional and physical closeness.

PATIENCE: "PAUSE AND BREATHE CHALLENGE"

Activity: Try the "Pause and Breathe Challenge." When faced with a moment of frustration, commit to pausing, taking three deep breaths, and then calmly discussing your feelings. Afterward, acknowledge how the pause helped both of you.

Why It Reduces Tension: Practicing patience prevents conflicts from escalating.

How It Builds Trust: Responding with patience shows respect and commitment to understanding each other.

Q

QUALITY TIME

Moments that are shared between a husband and a wife where they give each other undivided attention is called quality time. Most marriages are riddled with all sorts of distractions, but the biggest one of all are the devices we hold in our hands, the cell phone. A wife who spends time getting ready for a night out with her husband only to be overshadowed by the fluorescent glow on his face can be disappointing. A husband who desperately needs his wife, but she is constantly pulled away by text messages and social media updates can cause him to feel the same way. There must be a time where both the husband and wife agree to put the phone down and spend time with each other looking eye to eye. There should be nothing more entertaining or exciting than a wife staring into her husband's eyes over dinner or a husband touching his wife's hand during dessert. Song of Solomon 1:15 describes it this way "your eyes are dove's eyes." A dove is known to be keenly focused and sharp in their vision. The only thing they look at is what they want in the moment. May your quality time be spent looking only at one another.

QUENCH

There are moments when difficulties seems to flood your marriage. A wife can feel like she is drowning in disappointment. The husband can feel like he is holding on to broken pieces of his career. Financial pressure is beginning to leak into your home. A tidal wave of commitments with the kids can try to pull you under. But when a couple can come together and encourage one another that they will make it out together, the waters of life will start to subside. Song of Solomon 8:7 says, "many waters cannot quench love." When struggling with the floods of life, the love between the husband and wife cannot be put out. It is the power that keeps them afloat, no matter what.

QUIT

A husband and wife should have the mentality that quitting is not an option. It is not abnormal to want to resign from being a couple, but the permanency of that decision must be weighed. It may seem that the best answer to difficulty is to stop facing it together. The plan of the enemy is to kill, steal, and destroy. He is not after material things; he is after your marriage. Tension between a husband and a wife can stretch them to the point of snapping in two! Deception will say that the only way to relieve the pressure is to give up and quit. But then a couple has already decided that ending their marriage is not an option, there will be a tenacity that will cause them to stick and stay. Galatians 6:9 says, "and let us not grow weary of doing good, for in due season we will reap is we do not give up." A husband and wife who remind each other that doing good can be tiresome and that their due season is coming, will enjoy the fruit of their labor together.

Q

Activities

QUALITY TIME: "TECH-FREE EVENING"

Activity: Plan a "Tech-Free Evening." Turn off all devices for a few hours and spend uninterrupted time together. Play a game, cook a meal, or simply talk about your day. Focus entirely on each other.

Why It Strengthens Connection: Uninterrupted time allows you to truly focus on each other and build intimacy.

How It Fosters Closeness: Shared experiences deepen your bond and create lasting memories.

QUENCH: "LOVE REFRESH SESSION"

Activity: Have a "Love Refresh Session." Sit down together and ask, "What can I do to refresh and quench your emotional or physical needs right now?" Take turns fulfilling one small request, like a compliment, a hug, or an act of service.

Why It Recharges Love: Meeting each other's needs directly shows care and attentiveness.

How It Encourages Communication: Openly asking and responding fosters emotional connection and satisfaction.

QUIT: "FRESH START CONVERSATION"

Activity: Practice a "Fresh Start Conversation." Choose a quiet moment to talk about something you both agree to quit, like interrupting during conversations or bringing up past mistakes. Make a pact to support each other in building better habits, and end the conversation with a hug or a toast to new beginnings.

Why It Promotes Growth: Openly addressing habits helps create a healthier dynamic.

How It Strengthens Partnership: Working together to improve fosters mutual support and accountability.

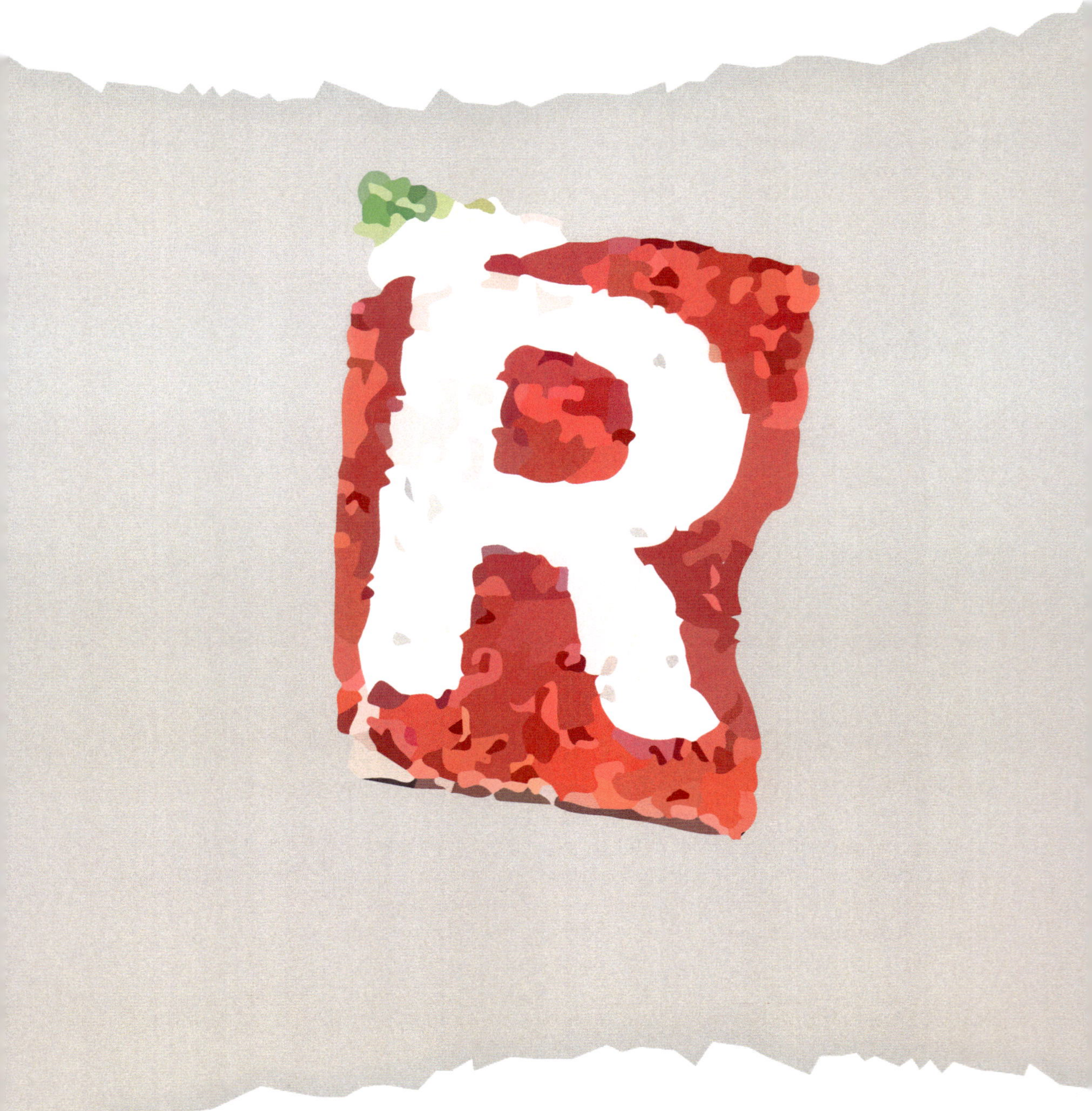
R

RECONCILE

Disagreements can cause a couple to no longer feel like friends. This happens when the husband or wife are not willing to adjust, adapt, or agree to disagree. If the contention lasts a long time, it could begin to effect communication, consideration, and connectivity. Just because there are differs of opinions on a topic doesn't mean that you cannot get along. There should be a moment when either the husband or wife makes the decision to reconcile. This means, one of the two must be the bigger person and try to get back on friendly terms. Once that happens by either party, the one that is holding out must quickly accept the peace offering. Reconciliation must be between the husband and the wife. 2 Corinthians 5:18 "…Christ reconciled us to himself and gave us the ministry of reconciliation." Making an effort to get back on friendly terms is possible because Jesus did the same thing for us.

REST

The life between a husband and wife should not just be one of schedules, appointments, and obligations. There should be a set time where the husband and wife find time to rest. It is easy for the relationship to become neglected because priorities became out of order. Productivity may feel good, but a peaceful day of rest and relaxation feels better especially with the one you love. There should be one day a week where time off is accepted and practiced. This could mean a quiet Sunday afternoon (after church) at home or a quick road trip out of town for a change of scenery. The goal is to make sure you both feel relaxed and achieve the goal of rest. Matthew 11:28, " Come to me, all who labor and are heavy laden, and I will give you rest." A couple who can find rest in the Lord will have no problem finding rest with each other.

RELATIONSHIPS

A husband and wife should be each other's best friend. There should be no one closer to either person. They should have balanced relationship with their children, understanding that they did not make a covenant with their kids.

Although there are moments when children need time and attention, the husband and wife should have balance with keeping the health of their marriage a priority. Parents, in-laws and siblings should also accept boundaries that have been set in place by the word of God to ensure a healthy marriage.

It is also healthy for a husband and wife to have a set of like-minded friends that support the same values and honor marriage. The most important relationship a husband and wife should have is their personal relationship with Jesus.

Activities

RECONCILE: "RECONNECTION WALK"

Activity: Plan a "Reconnection Walk." Take a walk together in a peaceful setting and discuss one area where you may feel distant or disconnected. Use this time to listen to each other's feelings and brainstorm ways to rebuild closeness.

Why It Fosters Healing: Open communication in a calm environment encourages resolution and understanding.

How It Strengthens Trust: Rebuilding connection shows your commitment to the relationship's growth.

REST: "RELAXATION NIGHT"

Activity: Create a "Relaxation Night." Plan a stress-free evening with soothing activities, like watching a favorite movie, enjoying a warm bath together, or sharing a quiet meal. Set rules to avoid heavy topics—just relax and enjoy each other's company.

Why It Promotes Peace: Taking time to rest together recharges your emotional and physical energy.

How It Deepens Bonding: Shared relaxation moments reinforce comfort and safety in your relationship.

RELATIONSHIPS: "RELATIONSHIP GOALS CHAT"

Activity: Host a "Relationship Goals Chat." Sit down and talk about what's working well in your relationship and one goal you'd like to work on as a team. Make it fun by turning it into a mini brainstorming session with snacks and drinks.

Why It Encourages Growth: Reflecting on your relationship's strengths and goals strengthens its foundation.

How It Builds Alignment: Working toward shared goals fosters teamwork and deeper emotional connection.

S

SENTIMENTAL

A husband and wife that are strongly influenced by positive feelings, especially about happy memories of past events, are considered a sentimental couple. Occasionally looking back and remembering tender moments of the good times you have shared together can reaffirm why you have stayed together. This is also a way to connect as you relive pastime enjoyment and pleasure. Talking about how you met, your first date, or the moment you fell in love will pull on your heart strings and cause you to reminisce. Reminiscing is said to benefit a couple's mental health because it is a recall of positive memories that can ignite past feelings of love and happiness. I will remember the works of the Lord ; surely I will remember Your wonders of old. I will also meditate on all of Your work and talk of Your deeds Psalm 77:11-12

SOUL MATE

A soul mate is often crafted more than found. This means that a deep connection with your spouse can be created over time. It is someone you feel deeply connected to but not in a dependent way. A husband and wife need to have a connection deeper than an infatuation. Remaining married must be more than a short-lived passion that can present as something deeper. Saying your husband or wife is your soul mate means that you help each other grow, have mutual empathy, and share steadfast love. Growth is the key component in the relationship. The more experiences you share, good and bad, the more bonded you will become. Loving one another during different stages of life develops a love that is unconditional. When a husband and wife are emotionally and spiritually connected, they can fulfill Genesis 2:24 …and they shall become one flesh.

SEX

Sex between husband and wife is honored by God. The marriage bed is pure and desire for your spouse is encouraged. God designed sexual activity to be enjoyed as husband and wife. He encourages the couple to sexually satisfy one another in creative and unique ways. The joy of marriage is when you are willing to unselfishly give to your spouse, not just for procreation, but for sheer pleasure. Withholding sex from your spouse leaves him or her unprotected and open to physical or emotional temptations that can devastate a marriage. The only time a couple should abstain from sexual intercourse is only for an agreed, short time of fasting. Marital sex is a way to reconnect and rebuild the relationship, especially when going through difficult times. A deeper bond is created when a married couple regularly enjoys intimacy that both satisfies and fulfills sexual needs. Proverbs 5:18-19, Song of Solomon 4:9-11, Hebrews 13:4

S

Activities

SENTIMENTAL: "MILESTONE CELEBRATION"

Activity: Plan a "Milestone Celebration." Pick a meaningful moment from your relationship, like your first date or a favorite trip, and recreate it with small details—similar meals, music, or locations. Reflect on how far you've come and what made that moment special.

Why It Strengthens Connection: Reliving cherished memories reinforces the emotional bond between you.

How It Builds Appreciation: Celebrating milestones highlights the growth and depth of your relationship.

SOUL MATE: "LOVE VOWS 2.0"

Activity: Write "Love Vows 2.0." Each partner takes a few minutes to create new vows that reflect where you are in your relationship today. Share them during a candlelit moment, reaffirming your unique connection as soulmates.

Why It Rekindles Passion: Reaffirming your bond in meaningful words strengthens emotional intimacy.

How It Celebrates Connection: Acknowledging your soulmate connection renews love and commitment.

SEX: "SENSORY EXPERIENCE NIGHT"

Activity: Plan a "Sensory Experience Night." Set the mood with soft lighting, scented candles, music, and comfortable textures to create a relaxing and intimate atmosphere. Take turns exploring each other's preferences through conversation, touch, and thoughtful gestures.

Why It Builds Intimacy: Engaging all senses creates a deeper physical and emotional connection.

How It Enhances Closeness: Focusing on each other's desires fosters trust, passion, and a stronger bond.

T

TIME

A husband who makes time for his wife is a man who understands priority and effort. When a wife is treated as more important than everything else, she will feel appreciated and loved. Understanding that time is the most valuable assets given to man, carving it out for your husband will be seen as a sacrifice. Life brings changes where time must be shared when it comes to children, work schedules, and personal plans. But making your marriage priority is still vital for the strength and survival of the union. When time is managed in a way that makes the husband and wife feel important, there will be compatibility and understanding, especially when intentional attempts are made to make it happen. Ephesians 5:16 says to make the best use of time. When a couple spends time together, it only solidifies the bond between husband and wife. Time together is time well spent.

TRUST

When a wife trusts her husband, she has a firm belief in his ability, reliability, and truth of his character. She will have confidence in his role in her life and in turn will find confidence in her role as his wife. A husband who can trust his wife is a man who know she will do him good all of his days and not bring him harm (Proverbs 31:12).

When a couple is certain in their relationship, they become determined to remain together. Tenacity, the ability to remain persistent, is built on trust; it is the motivation to continue building a life together as a unit. Although trust can be broken in a marriage, it can be rebuilt. Jeremiah 32:27 asks this, "is there anything too hard for God?". Trusting the Lord to fulfill His word is the first step to rebuilding trust in the marriage.

THOUGHTFUL

A thoughtful wife is a woman who remembers what her husband needs, wants, or feels. She is a partner who tries to not upset her husband on purpose. Because women are naturally observant, she can pick up on body language and social cues her mate is consciously or subconsciously giving.

A husband who is thoughtful will not just hear but will remember what his wife prefers or enjoys.   Thoughtfulness is having consideration for one another with intentionality.   It goes beyond being kind because it takes the key word, thought, to put forth and effort. When a husband and wife are thinking about each other often, thoughtfulness will be seen often as well.

Ephesians 4:32 reminds us to be kind to one another. Being thoughtful is an exaggerated form of kindness.

T

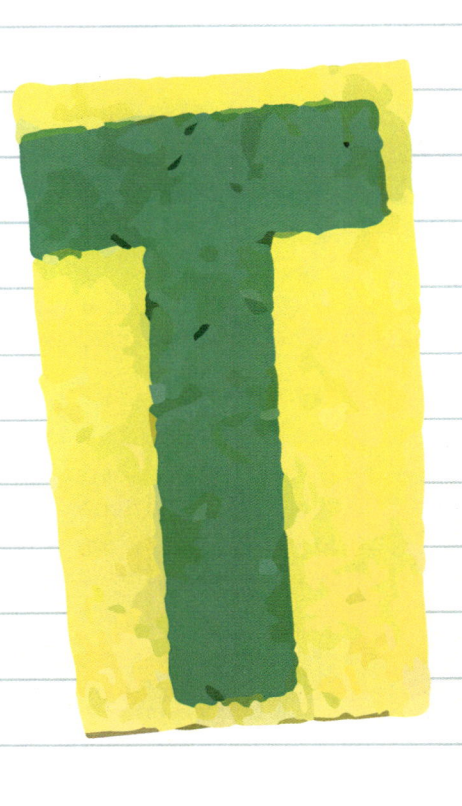

Activities

TIME: "HEARTFELT PLAYLIST"

Activity: Create a "Mini Daycation." Dedicate a half-day to disconnect from distractions and spend uninterrupted time together. Whether it's a picnic at a park, a stroll through a museum, or relaxing at home, make the focus solely on enjoying each other's company.

Why It Strengthens Connection: Prioritizing focused time together deepens emotional intimacy and understanding.

How It Recharges the Relationship: Stepping away from daily routines revitalizes your bond and creates lasting memories.

TRUST: "QUESTION ROULETTE"

Activity: Play the "Truth and Trust Game." Each partner asks the other a lighthearted or meaningful question they've always wanted to know. Answer with honesty and openness, using the moment to deepen understanding.

Why It Builds Security: Open dialogue reinforces honesty and transparency in the relationship.

How It Deepens Respect: Sharing truths fosters vulnerability and strengthens emotional intimacy.

THOUGHTFUL: "FUTURE GOALS ADVENTURE"

Activity: Plan a "Custom Care Package." Gather a few small items that remind you of your spouse's interests or things they've mentioned needing (e.g., their favorite snack, a meaningful book, or a handwritten note). Present it as a surprise to show you've been paying attention.

Why It Shows Care: Tailoring a gesture to their preferences demonstrates attentiveness and love.

How It Enhances Bonding: Thoughtful surprises reinforce emotional connection and appreciation.

U

UNDERSTANDING

The bible instructs a husband that he should live with his with understanding for she is the weaker vessel (1 Peter 3:7). This means that he should foster a relationship that is sympathetically aware of his wife's feelings. He has the responsibility to be tolerant with her emotions and even forgiving for her actions, if need be. The wife being the weaker vessel doesn't mean that she is not as strong as the man. It means that she is not able to contain as much as he.

When a wife reaches her limit mentally or emotionally, her husband should be the one to respond to her by comfort and assurance, not frustration or criticism. When a wife feels understood by the man she loves, she may have 'moments', but they will be short-lived.

UNITED

A husband and wife who live a united life are a couple who walk in harmony. They are both in agreement with where they are currently and where they are headed in the future. They are both careful to watch their personal connections to make certain threats are pointed out that may cause division between their union.

Because they understand that a house divided will not stand (Mark 3:25), they both make great efforts to walk together by strong communication with one another and especially with the Lord through prayer. A united couple understands and operates in the power of agreement. Matthew 18:19-20 says that if two of you agree about anything they ask for, it will be done for them by my Father. When a husband and wife come together in faith, the limits are removed by the power of God.

UPBEAT

A wife who is managing her home well, raising her children, and working may find it difficult to remain cheerful, but having a cheerful disposition makes a world of difference. A husband depends on her optimism especially when doubt is lingering.

When the wife is upbeat, she can keep a steady rhythm of laughter and love in the home. Refusing to take everything seriously can sometimes feel like a lack of responsibility, but it keeps the temperature mild and welcoming. Positivity is a powerful attribute because it sways outcomes and makes life more tolerable. It can cause a feeling of calmness and well-being no matter what may currently be going on. Proverbs 15:13 says a cheerful heart makes a cheerful face. The more a wife smiles, the more comfort she brings to her spouse. All because she has made the choice to remain upbeat.

U

Activities

UNDERSTANDING: "EMPATHY HOUR"

Activity: Have an "Empathy Hour." Take turns sharing a recent experience or challenge, and the other partner practices active listening by reflecting back what they hear and how they imagine it felt. End by sharing one way you can support each other moving forward.

Why It Builds Empathy: Taking time to truly understand each other fosters emotional intimacy.

How It Strengthens Trust: Feeling heard and supported deepens the bond between you.

UNITED: "TEAMWORK CHALLENGE"

Activity: Plan a "Teamwork Challenge." Pick a fun activity that requires collaboration, like cooking a new recipe together, assembling furniture, or tackling a DIY project. Celebrate your success with a high-five and a shared treat.

Why It Encourages Teamwork: Working together reinforces your ability to face challenges as a united front.

How It Builds Partnership: Shared accomplishments strengthen your sense of being on the same team.

UPBEAT: "POSITIVITY PLAYLIST"

Activity: Create a "Positivity Playlist." Each partner selects their favorite cheerful songs, and together, make a playlist to listen to during a shared activity like cooking, cleaning, or driving. Sing along or dance to your favorite tracks to keep the energy high and joyful.

Why It Boosts Mood: Music naturally lifts spirits and creates a fun, shared experience.

How It Builds Connection: Sharing and enjoying each other's favorite songs fosters a sense of togetherness and playfulness.

VACATION

A husband and wife should try to regularly schedule time away. It is a period where the routine is stopped, and quality time is spent with one another. It is also a time to create new memories and enjoy new experiences together. Sometimes a marriage needs a change of scenery to put a little gas on the flame of love. When times away are planned, in advance, the couple can budget and work together to save the money it will cost to get away.

This is a way to enjoy the fruit of your labor because you are working for a purpose. There is nothing wrong with scheduling a time of rest. Even God rested on the seventh day (Genesis 2:3)

VISIONARY

A husband who is a leader will be a visionary for his wife and family. A wife, in turn, will be a visionary for the home. When a husband has a vision for his family, he has an idea of what it will take to provide for them. He is a man who walks in wisdom and plans for their future.

A wife will use her imagination and creativity to provide a beautiful and loving home environment. A couple who has vision for their marriage will have a strong idea of what the future will look like, especially how it will be improved.

Without a vision, there is no direction (Habukkuk 2:2)

VULNERABILITY

Vulnerability is another form of intimacy. A wife who is vulnerable is a woman who is not afraid to share her true feelings without the threat of being hurt. A husband who is emotionally open with his wife is a man who trusts his heart with her. Each know that special care is given when private thoughts are shared. They both trust that their "pillow talk" will never become public.

The risk of being wounded with personal information is completely removed when vulnerable moments are kept private. When you are vulnerable with the Lord by confessing sin (admitting your faults and fears), the bible says that He provides strength and healing (James 5:16). When you go to the one you love in the same way, the same should be provided.

V

Activities

VACATION: "STAYCATION ADVENTURE"

Activity: Plan a "Staycation Adventure." Transform your home or local area into a mini getaway. Set a theme (like beach day or city escape), cook themed meals, and schedule activities like watching travel documentaries or exploring a nearby attraction.

Why It Recharges Energy: Breaking from routine brings excitement and a sense of relaxation.

How It Strengthens Bonding: Shared adventures, even at home, create lasting memories and a sense of fun.

VISIONARY: "DREAM BIG NIGHT"

Activity: Host a "Dream Big Night." Take turns sharing your biggest dreams and visions for your life together—whether it's travel goals, career aspirations, or family plans. Sketch out a timeline or create a visual representation of these dreams.

Why It Inspires Growth: Thinking big as a couple reinforces shared ambitions and future alignment.

How It Builds Excitement: Dreaming together creates anticipation and a shared sense of purpose.

VULNERABILITY: "DEEP QUESTIONS GAME"

Activity: Play the "Deep Questions Game." Take turns asking each other open-ended questions like, "What's something you've never told me?" or "What's a fear you've overcome recently?" Focus on listening without judgment and offering support.

Why It Encourages Trust: Being open and vulnerable strengthens emotional intimacy.

How It Deepens Connection: Sharing fears, hopes, and personal stories fosters closeness and understanding.

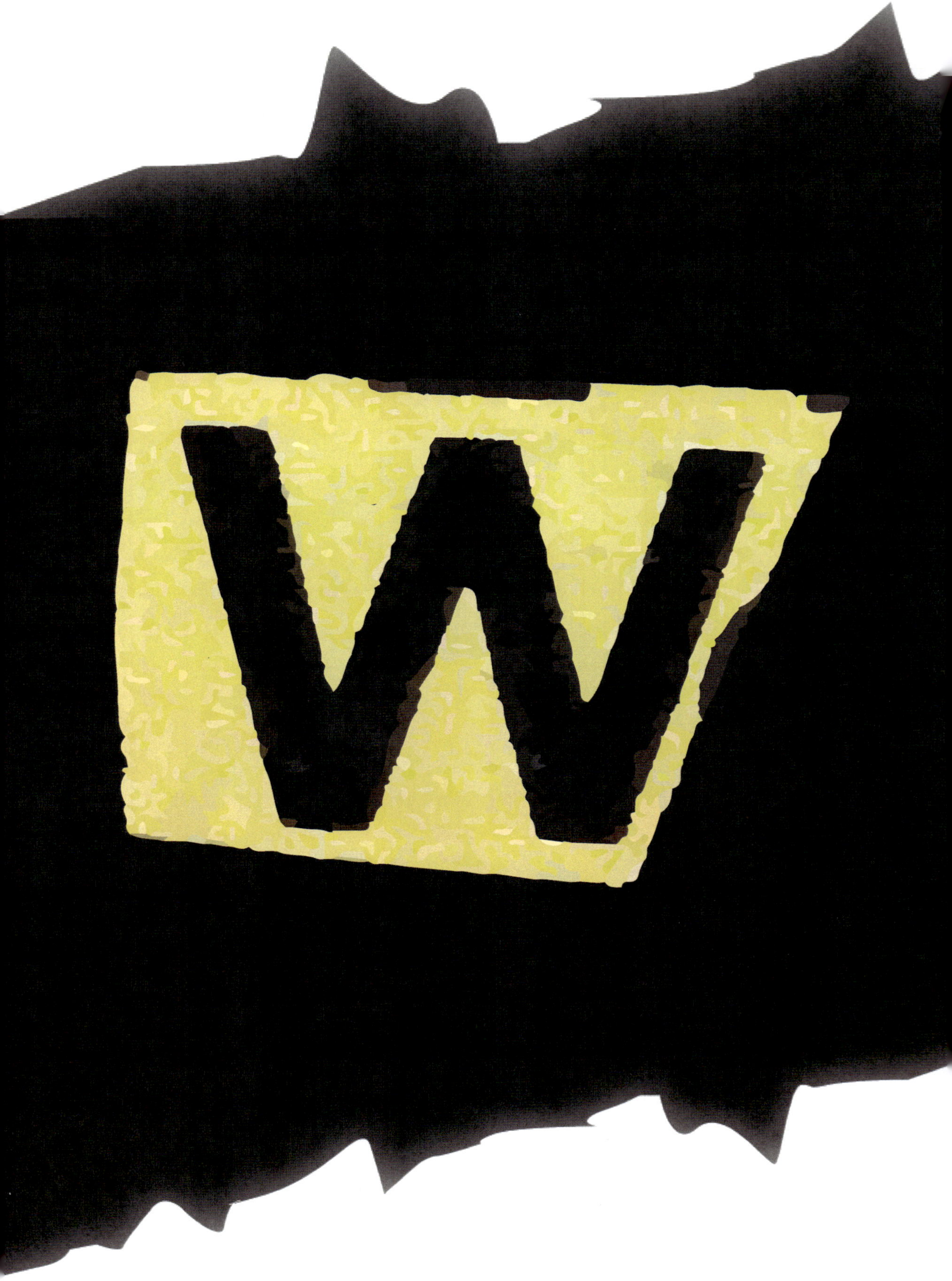
W

WISDOM

When a husband and wife depend on the wisdom of God, they are a couple who trust the Lord to know the greatest way to approach a situation. They know that the foolishness of God is wiser than human wisdom (1 Corinthians 1:25). Therefore, they look to His guidance according to the word of God and with prayer. This couple values wise counsel and advice.

They not only are receptive, but they are reciprocates fueling one another with good instructions. Because they are not quick to react, they depend on wisdom before they respond to situations. Humility is the core of their belief that allows them to reverence the Lord, which is the beginning of wisdom (Proverbs 15:33).

WORK

A good husband is a man who is willing to work to provide for his wife. He is not afraid to put in time to make an honest living to care for those he is responsible for. He strives to ensure a stable income is provided to make a comfortable life for his bride. The wife is also willing to work to make sure the home is provided for. It doesn't matter if it is outside of the home or inside the home, labor is necessary from both the husband and wife if they want to build a life together.

They find fulfillment working outside of the home, but they also enjoy working in the home together. Creating plans and completing projects brings a sense of purpose for the hard work that was put forth to reach a goal. They also understand that after hard work comes a time to enjoy the fruit of their labor together (Psalm 128:2).

WEALTH

When a couple has an abundance of money or valuable possessions, they are considered wealthy. They have amassed an unlimited number of resources, but true wealth is much more than material or monetary things. They are a couple who has an abundance of love, joy, and peace.

This is a deeper aspect of what is valuable that exceeds physical wealth; it is spiritual. The bible says in 3 John 1:2 "….I pray that in every way you may prosper and enjoy good health and that all may go well with you as your soul is getting along well."

It is the will of God that the life of a husband and wife is expected to have an abundance of love for one another, feelings of happiness, and continued calmness. This type of wealth is not only generational, but also eternal.

W

Activities

WISDOM: "LIFE LESSONS NIGHT"

Activity: Plan a "Life Lessons Night." Share with each other the most valuable lessons you've learned in life or in your relationship. Reflect on how these lessons have shaped you as individuals and as a couple, and discuss how you can apply them moving forward.

Why It Encourages Growth: Exchanging wisdom promotes learning and mutual respect.

How It Builds Understanding: Reflecting on past experiences deepens your connection and insight into each other's journey.

WORK: "WORK BUDDY HOUR"

Activity: Plan a "Work Buddy Hour." Set aside time to work on individual tasks side by side, whether it's catching up on emails, planning, or creative projects. Offer each other small acts of support, like making a coffee or giving encouraging words during breaks.

Why It Promotes Teamwork: Supporting each other while working fosters a sense of partnership.

How It Strengthens Connection: Sharing space and encouragement builds camaraderie and mutual appreciation.

WEALTH: "WEALTH VISION BOARD"

Activity: Try a "Wealth Vision Board." Spend time creating a board that represents your financial goals as a couple. Include images or words symbolizing saving, investing, or traveling, and discuss actionable steps to reach these goals together.

Why It Promotes Alignment: Visualizing and discussing financial dreams ensures you're on the same page.

How It Builds Trust: Collaborative planning shows a shared commitment to building a prosperous future.

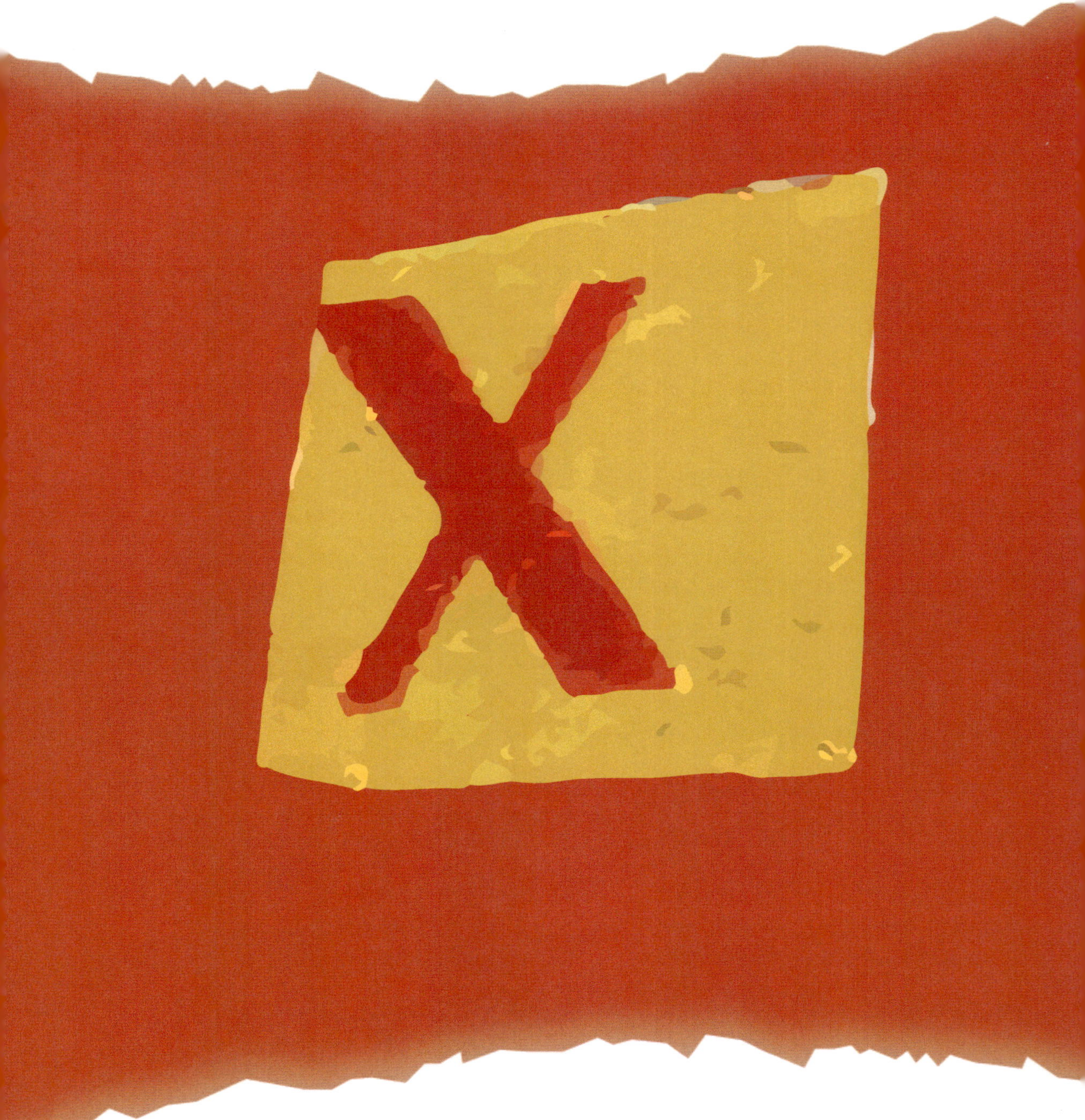
X

XENIAL

A married couple should be friendly and warm to guests, especially when they enter their home. Hosting visitors is a way extending the love you have for one another to others. Hospitality helps build strong relationships and creates a sense of community to all.

When a husband and wife are friendly and welcoming to each other, it is easy for them to extend the same to strangers. When a couple is known for having a warm, embracing disposition toward others, they exemplify the love of Christ. 1 Peter 4:9 says to show hospitality to one another without grumbling. When husband and wife can extend friendliness to one another without complaining, they can organically do the same for others.

X-FACTOR

When a husband and wife can recognize something unique in each another, they have found their partners "x-factor". It is that quality that may not be easily explainable but makes them very special. Exceptional qualities are what made them attractive in the first place.

It is important that this quality isn't forgotten or wane down by familiarity. When that special something is displayed, a wife should complement her husband. When a husband is reminded of the exquisite quality that caught his attention in the first place, he should let her know.

That one thing that makes your spouse special is an example of how God has "wonderfully and fearfully"(Psalm 139:14) created him or her especially for you.

XOXO

Kisses and hugs are vital for a marriage to thrive. Mutual affection is a physical response to having a tender attachment to one another. A full embrace should last 15 seconds for a connection to be felt. Kissing releases endorphins and brain calming chemicals that reduce stress. It

makes you feel connected and secure within the marital relationship. When a husband and wife take time to share tender affection, without sexual intercourse, it creates a long lasting bond.

Song of Solomon 1:2 says : "Let him kiss me with the kisses of His mouth. For your love is better than wine." Hugging and kissing can truly make you drunk in love.

Activities

XENIAL: "HOSPITALITY NIGHY IN"

Activity: Plan a "Hospitality Night In." Host a cozy dinner for just the two of you, complete with thoughtful touches like a beautifully set table, handwritten place cards, and a special dessert. Treat each other like honored guests.

Why It Promotes Warmth: Creating a welcoming atmosphere encourages mutual appreciation.

How It Strengthens Connection: Thoughtful gestures show care and foster a sense of being cherished.

X-FACTOR: "COUPLE'S SUPERPOWER"

Activity: Discover Your "Couple's Superpower." Spend time identifying what makes your relationship unique—whether it's your humor, teamwork, or shared dreams. Write it down or give it a fun nickname, and celebrate it by doing something that highlights that trait together.

Why It Inspires Confidence: Recognizing your strengths as a couple reinforces your bond.

How It Builds Pride: Emphasizing your uniqueness celebrates the special connection you share.

XOXO: "HUGS & KISSES COUNTDOWN"

Activity: Try a "Hugs & Kisses Countdown." Set a timer for five minutes and take turns giving each other hugs, kisses, or playful touches. Keep it light, affectionate, and fun to bring a spark of joy into your day.

Why It Rekindles Affection: Simple, physical closeness strengthens emotional and physical intimacy.

How It Deepens Bonding: Prioritizing affectionate moments creates warmth and connection. Hugging and kissing can truly make you drunk in love.

у

YIELD

A wife who is submitted to her husband is a woman who has made the decision to yield to his authority. She is okay with giving way or surrendering her will to the will of her spouse. It takes yielding because a wife is to follow her husband as the spiritual leader of the home as he makes Christ-like decisions.

This does not mean she doesn't have an opinion or should not have a voice in certain matters. It means that if there are opposing views, the husband has the right to make the final decision. The bible is clear that a wife should submit to her own husband while the husband is to love his wife.

(Ephesians 5:22-23) A yielded wife should expect love in return.

YEARN

A husband who has an intense longing for his wife, especially after being separated for a while, is called yearning. Even after years of being together, it is healthy to long for the companionship of your spouse. Having a desire for the one you love is an indication that the fire is still burning strong in the relationship. There is nothing wrong with a wife longing to be intimate with her husband.

Sexual desire is evident with the craving to intimately enjoy one another. Song of Solomon 3:1-2 describes it like this: "I yearned for my lover, but he did not come. So, I said to myself, "I will get up and roam the city, searching in all its streets and squares. I will search for the one I love." Yearning will make you get up and look for the only one who can satisfy your craving, your spouse.

YOKED

When a husband a wife is connected, they can be considered yoked together. A natural yoke is a harness used to connect two oxen or other animals to pull a cart. This apparatus is intended to keep the oxen united in step and is also to make a heavy load lighter. It is also there to help guide the animals in the right direction. Saying a married couple are yoked is saying that they are attached by God and are to remain in step with His purpose. It also says that two are better than one because it makes difficult burdens easier to carry.

Lastly, a couple who is yoked together by God will be kept going in the right direction as they are guided by his divine direction. Matthew 11:28-30 says that we can come to Jesus because his yoke is easy and His burden is light. When couple is joined together with Christ, He will make the work in the marriage easier to manage and definite to succeed.

y

Activities

YIELD: "YOUR TURN GAME"

Activity: Play the "Your Turn Game." Spend an evening letting your spouse take the lead in choosing activities, meals, or entertainment for the day. Practice yielding graciously to their preferences and enjoy seeing what brings them joy.

Why It Builds Harmony: Giving space to your partner's preferences strengthens balance and mutual respect.

How It Encourages Growth: Learning to yield creates a partnership built on understanding and compromise.

YEARN: "DREAM TOGETHER NIGHT"

Activity: Plan a "Dream Together Night." Talk about what you long for in your relationship or life—whether it's adventures, deeper connections, or shared goals. Use this time to visualize how you can bring those desires to life as a team.

Why It Deepens Emotional Intimacy: Sharing your deepest desires creates vulnerability and trust.

How It Builds Connection: Yearning together aligns your dreams and strengthens your shared vision for the future.

YOKED: "STRENGTHS AND STRUGGLE LIST"

Activity: Create a "Strengths and Struggles List." As a couple, identify areas where you're strongest together and where you might need more support. Discuss how you can yoke your strengths to overcome struggles and build a stronger partnership.

Why It Promotes Unity: Recognizing your strengths and challenges reinforces teamwork.

How It Strengthens Partnership: Working together to balance each other's weaknesses fosters mutual support and commitment.

Z

ZEALOUS

A married couple who is devoted to one another will show it with great enthusiasm called zeal. Their fervent love will be hard to hide. They will wholeheartedly remain committed and excited about the relationship. Even as the years pass by, they will spend time and energy supporting one another to win. They will both want good things for them personally and spiritually.

Family is the cause they are devoted to. This zealous love will keep the couple reciprocating mercy so they can remain husband and wife for the rest of their lives. 1 Peter 4:8 "Above all, love each other deeply, because love covers over a multitude of sins."

ZONE

A zone is a place where a husband and wife reside in their personal space that has their character displayed. It is the area where mutual boundaries have been set. In other words, their home is their zone. If home is where the heart is, the home should reflect the heart of the husband and wife. It should be a place of peace and security. It should feel warm and inviting. It must also be considered sacred and limited to who comes in and who goes out. The zone should be protected with prayer and limited access.

2 Corinthians 13:11 says this, "Aim for restoration, comfort one another, agree with one another, live in peace; and the God of love and peace will be with you." When a husband and wife aim for mending their relationship, walking in agreement, and desire to live in tranquility, they have made their home their zone.

ZENITH

A husband and wife are the most powerful and successful when their relationship is in complete alignment with Jesus Christ. This is the zenith; the highest point a covenant relationship can go. A couple united in Christ can accomplish whatever they believe for, by faith. They can achieve the unachievable and do the impossible. A couple can solve problems easier; they can help each other by working together to figure situations out.

When two work together they will have a good reward for their labor (Ecclesiastes 4:9). Where 2 (or 3) are gathered in the name of Jesus, He is there (Matthew 18:20). If husband and wife agree on earth about anything, it will be done by the Father in heaven (Matthew 18:18-19). A couple who is willing and obedient to the word of God will eat the good of the land together. (Isaiah 1:19) Marching together in agreement to the heartbeat of God will pour out power and surround your life with success.

Z

Activities

ZEALOUS: "PASSION PURSUIT DATE"

Activity: Plan a "Passion Pursuit Date." Choose an activity that excites both of you—whether it's trying a thrilling sport, attending a lively event, or diving into a shared hobby. Commit to enjoying the experience with enthusiasm and energy.

Why It Sparks Joy: Sharing passions brings energy and excitement into your relationship.

How It Builds Connection: Pursuing interests with zeal deepens your bond and creates lasting memories.

ZONE: "COMFORT ZONE CHALLENGE"

Activity: Create a "Comfort Zone Challenge." Take turns encouraging each other to step out of your comfort zones with small, fun challenges (e.g., trying a new food or speaking about something vulnerable). Cheer each other on throughout.

Why It Encourages Growth: Pushing boundaries together fosters courage and mutual support.

How It Strengthens Trust: Being there for each other in challenging moments reinforces your partnership.

ZENITH: "PEAK MOMENT NIGHT"

Activity: Celebrate a "Peak Moment Night." Reflect on and celebrate a high point in your relationship—like a big milestone, a special trip, or a shared accomplishment. Recreate the mood or memory with photos, stories, and favorite treats from that time.

Why It Builds Gratitude: Reliving peak moments reminds you of the strength and beauty of your relationship.

How It Inspires Future Goals: Reflecting on achievements motivates you to strive for new shared zeniths.

Made in the USA
Columbia, SC
03 May 2025

034959b7-8700-4730-a8af-cf0d78508e1fR01